Max Stone

The Awakening of Abundance
A Spiritual Journey to Achieve Dreams

Original Title: O Despertar da Abundância

Copyright © 2024, published by Luiz Antonio dos Santos ME.

This book is a work of non-fiction that explores practices and concepts in the field of personal development and abundance. Through a comprehensive approach, the author offers practical tools to achieve emotional balance, prosperity, and personal fulfillment.

1st Edition
Production Team

Author: Max Stone
Editor: Luiz Santos
Cover: Studios Booklas/ Anselmo Mendes
Layout: Silvia Regis
Translation: Arnaldo Correa

Publication and Identification
The Awakening of Abundance
Editora Booklas, 2025
Categories: Personal Development / Spirituality / Prosperity
DDC: 158.1 - CDU: 159.923.2

All rights reserved to:
Luiz Antonio dos Santos ME / Booklas
No part of this book may be reproduced, stored in a retrieval system, or transmitted by any means — electronic, mechanical, photocopy, recording, or other — without the prior and express permission of the copyright holder.

Summary

Prologue 5
Chapter 1 Defining Abundance 8
Chapter 2 Positive Thoughts 15
Chapter 3 Powerful Affirmations 23
Chapter 4 Creative Visualization 31
Chapter 5 The Law of Attraction 39
Chapter 6 Eliminating Limiting Beliefs 47
Chapter 7 Deep Self-Knowledge 55
Chapter 8 Inner Healing 63
Chapter 9 Abundance Mindset 71
Chapter 10 Positive Language 78
Chapter 11 Energy Cleansing 86
Chapter 12 Crystals and Abundance 93
Chapter 13 Vibrational Aromatherapy 100
Chapter 14 Feng Shui for Prosperity 108
Chapter 15 Music and Frequencies 116
Chapter 16 Meditation for Abundance 124
Chapter 17 Powerful Mantras 132
Chapter 18 Sacred Mudras 140
Chapter 19 Dance and Movement 147
Chapter 20 Energy Baths 155
Chapter 21 Color Visualization 163
Chapter 22 Continuous Learning 171
Chapter 23 Giving and Sharing 179
Chapter 24 Creating Opportunities 187

Chapter 25 Celebrating Success 195
Chapter 26 Attitude of Gratitude 203
Chapter 27 Visualizing the Future 210
Chapter 28 Acting with Intuition 217
Chapter 29 Spiritual Connection 225
Chapter 30 Serving the World 232
Chapter 31 Following your Intuition 239
Chapter 32 Living with Purpose 247
Chapter 33 Material Detachment 255
Chapter 34 Simplicity and Minimalism 263
Chapter 35 Inner Abundance 270
Chapter 36 Sharing Abundance 278
Epilogue 285

Prologue

Dear reader,

You are about to embark on a journey that transcends the pages of a simple book. This is not just a compendium of words; it is an invitation to dive into a universe where true abundance is not just a concept, but a living, pulsating, and transformative experience.

We live in a world saturated with superficial ideas about success and prosperity, where abundance is often confused with material accumulation. But what if I told you that there is something much deeper, a hidden path that leads to a full life in all dimensions — mental, emotional, physical, and spiritual? Here, you will find that path.

As you turn these pages, you will not only read, but feel. You will feel the awakening of a new consciousness, where each word acts as a key to open previously invisible doors. This book whispers truths that remain hidden from inattentive eyes, but reveal themselves to those who have the courage to question, reflect, and transform.

Allow yourself to discover.

Imagine for a moment a life in which your actions flow in perfect harmony with your thoughts and emotions. Where fear no longer dictates your decisions and limiting beliefs dissolve like mist in the sun. This state is not a distant utopia — it is within your reach, closer than you imagine.

Here, you will learn that true abundance begins with mental clarity, emotional authenticity, and spiritual connection. These are not empty promises, but concrete practices that, when integrated into your routine, trigger real changes. Each concept explored has been carefully woven to provoke deep reflection, break self-sabotaging patterns, and rebuild a new perception of yourself and the world.

Are you ready for this awakening?

With each chapter, you will be guided to revisit your own history, your fears, your limitations. And, most importantly, you will be inspired to free yourself from them. This book is not an ordinary guide; it is a mirror that reflects not only who you are, but who you can be.

Imagine yourself walking through a lush garden where every flower, every leaf, every sound of nature resonates with the energy of abundance. This is the journey proposed here: a reconnection with the infinite source that sustains life, a natural harmony between giving and receiving, being and achieving.

Awaken. Abundance is not a privilege of a few. It is the right of all who choose to walk the path of self-knowledge and evolution. This book is more than reading; it is an experience of transformation. The words you will find here are seeds. And, as every good gardener knows, true beauty arises when cultivated with intention, patience, and love.

You have already taken the first step by opening this book. Now, allow yourself to dive in without reservation. Question. Reflect. Feel. And above all, allow yourself to be guided by each revelation that these pages have to offer.

May this reading be the beginning of a new stage, where every thought, every decision, every action is a reflection of your purest and most authentic essence.

Abundance awaits you.

Open this portal. Let yourself be led.

With deep admiration and trust,

Luiz Santos

Editor

Chapter 1
Defining Abundance

Abundance is the essence of a full and harmonious state that is reflected in all aspects of human existence, going beyond the accumulation of material goods. It is the expression of a life aligned with vibrant health, meaningful relationships, professional fulfillment, inner peace, and the freedom to live authentically. This state is characterized by a fluid connection with the universal source of prosperity and well-being, a dynamic balance that nourishes body, mind, and spirit. Thus, living in abundance does not just mean having enough to meet needs, but experiencing a fullness that transcends the very understanding of what is enough.

True abundance manifests itself in several interconnected dimensions, each contributing to a unified whole. In the material aspect, it is represented by financial security and the ability to enjoy the resources necessary for a comfortable life. Emotionally, it is the ability to express genuine feelings and cultivate relationships based on love, respect, and joy. In the mental field, abundance means possessing clarity, creativity, and the ability to learn continuously. On the spiritual plane, it lies in the deep connection with something greater, which brings meaning and purpose to life. Finally, physically, it is the vitality that comes from a healthy and balanced body.

Genuine prosperity is born from the recognition of the interconnection between these dimensions. Like pieces of a large mosaic, each area needs to be nurtured and balanced to form a complete picture of fullness. The mindset you adopt is a central piece in this process; positive thoughts, empowering beliefs, and a constant practice of gratitude create a fertile environment for abundance to flourish. Likewise, the energy you emanate, influenced by emotions and your vibration, connects with the energy around you, aligning your intentions with the opportunities that life offers.

Maintaining the balance between action and spirituality is equally essential to manifesting an abundant life. Action, guided by clarity of purpose and determination, is the channel through which your desires become reality. On the other hand, spiritual connection strengthens your trust in something greater, fueling your resilience and inspiration along the way. The integration of these daily practices forms the basis of a virtuous cycle of growth, where each achievement reinforces confidence and opens space for new possibilities.

The key to living in abundance lies in the conscious choice to align with this state. This requires self-knowledge to identify your genuine desires and overcome self-imposed limitations. Setting clear goals and acting purposefully is essential, as is practicing gratitude for everything that is already part of your life. With each step on this journey, you will be building an internal and external environment that favors continuous prosperity, allowing your life to be an authentic and vibrant expression of the fullness you deserve.

Imagine yourself walking through a lush garden, where nature flourishes in perfect harmony. Vibrant flowers bloom in vivid colors, fruit trees bend under the generous weight of their fruit, and a crystal-clear stream winds gently through the space, spreading freshness and serenity. Each element of this garden thrives at its own pace, coexisting in a balanced and natural way. This image is not just a metaphor for abundance, but a tangible representation of how life can be when we are aligned with the inexhaustible source of prosperity and well-being. Just as plants receive the right amount of light, water, and nutrients to grow, we too flourish when we nourish all areas of our existence.

This abundance manifests itself in different ways, starting with the material aspect. More than accumulating goods or money, true material abundance is living with enough financial prosperity to comfortably meet basic needs and, at the same time, fulfill personal desires. It brings security and freedom, allowing you to invest in your dreams and build a more balanced life. This state is achieved through conscious choices, such as solid financial planning, the practice of generosity, and the adoption of a growth mindset. Each responsible decision strengthens the roots of this security, allowing your projects to flourish naturally.

In the emotional field, abundance is revealed through the balance and authenticity with which you experience and express your feelings. Recognizing and accepting your emotions, whether joyful or challenging, without judgment, is the first step to cultivating deeper and more harmonious relationships. Developing self-love, empathy, and resilience strengthens this emotional foundation, creating an internal environment conducive to peace and joy. Daily gratitude and the enhancement of emotional intelligence function as essential nutrients for this form of abundance, nurturing emotional bonds and promoting well-being.

In the mental sphere, abundance translates into clarity of thought, creativity, and a mind open to continuous learning. An abundant mind is not limited by restrictive beliefs; on the contrary, it explores new ideas, questions paradigms, and adapts to changes with flexibility. To nurture this mental abundance, it is vital to constantly seek knowledge, reflect on experiences, stimulate curiosity, and balance moments of intense focus with periods of rest. Just as the earth needs to be turned over for new seeds to grow, the mind must be challenged and renewed to expand its possibilities.

The spiritual dimension of abundance transcends the material world, connecting you to something greater, whether through faith, meditation, contact with nature, or practices that awaken your life purpose. This deep connection brings a sense of belonging, inner peace, and alignment with core values. Spirituality nurtures compassion, gratitude, and the desire to serve, broadening your perception of yourself and the world around you. This alignment strengthens the foundation for a fulfilling life, guiding your choices and offering purpose to your actions.

Finally, physical abundance manifests itself in the vitality and health of the body. It is not just the absence of disease, but the vibrant energy that allows you to fully enjoy life. This state is built through nutritious food, regular exercise, restful sleep, and constant self-care. Just as a plant needs fertile soil, light, and water to grow, the body needs to be nourished and cared for to sustain the other aspects of abundance. Each healthy choice is an investment that increases your disposition and well-being.

True abundance, therefore, arises from the harmony between all these dimensions. Each aspect, like a piece of a puzzle, is fundamental to composing a full life. Nurturing each of these areas creates a solid foundation for prosperity to flourish in an integral way. This integration requires an adjusted mindset, where positive thoughts, empowering beliefs, and a constant practice of gratitude act as fertilizers for the soil of life. The energy you emanate, shaped by your emotions and intentions, interacts with the world around you, attracting opportunities aligned with your goals.

For this virtuous cycle of abundance to be maintained, it is essential to balance action and spirituality. Intentional action, guided by a clear purpose and determination, is the channel through which desires materialize. At the same time, spiritual connection nurtures trust in something greater, providing resilience and inspiration in the face of challenges. The daily integration of these practices creates a continuous flow of growth, where each achievement reinforces confidence and expands future possibilities.

Living in abundance requires a conscious choice of alignment with this state. This implies a deep dive into self-knowledge to identify genuine desires and break with self-imposed limitations. Setting clear goals and acting purposefully are fundamental steps, as is cultivating gratitude for what has already been achieved. Each conscious decision paves the way for an internal and external environment conducive to continuous prosperity, allowing your life to become an authentic expression of the fullness you deserve to experience.

By integrating these pillars into your life, you will be creating a virtuous cycle of abundance, where each area strengthens and contributes to your overall well-being. The journey towards abundance is a journey of self-discovery, growth, and transformation. It is an invitation to live a full life, aligned with your true essence and purpose.

Abundance is like a river that flows constantly, carrying with it the essence of renewal and infinite possibility. In order for this flow to remain uninterrupted, it is necessary to allow it to run its natural course, nourishing all areas of life. This involves accepting impermanence, trusting in cycles, and opening yourself to receive as much as to give. When you adopt this attitude of openness and surrender, abundance becomes more than a concept; it transforms into a tangible experience, a state of being that transcends the limitations of linear thinking.

By recognizing the interconnection between all forms of abundance, you realize that thriving is not a matter of accumulating, but of balancing. The harmony between the material, emotional, mental, spiritual, and physical aspects creates a magnetic field that attracts opportunities and achievements. This balance is neither rigid nor fixed; it constantly adjusts and renews itself, guided by your attention and intention. With each step you take, by aligning your actions with your deepest values, you contribute to this dynamic movement, strengthening the virtuous cycle of fullness.

Living in abundance is an act of courage and authenticity. It is trusting in the path that unfolds before you, even when it is not fully visible. It is celebrating small victories, learning from challenges, and continuing to move forward with faith. This journey, made of conscious and aligned choices, is the purest expression of human potential. When you connect with this energy, you not only transform your life, but also become a source of inspiration and prosperity for everyone around you.

Chapter 2
Positive Thoughts

The human mind doesn't just interpret the world around it; it plays an active role in creating the experiences we live. Each thought that emerges in our consciousness is like a piece of a grand mosaic, shaping the circumstances and results we experience. Instead of simply reacting to our environment, our thoughts project an energy that interacts with the possibilities around us, aligning events, opportunities, and even people with the essence of what we nurture mentally. This process occurs continuously and subtly, highlighting the importance of cultivating thought patterns that favor growth, positivity, and prosperity in our lives.

The strength of our thoughts can be compared to seeds sown in fertile ground. Each thought charged with hope, optimism, and gratitude is a seed that, upon finding prepared and nourished soil, germinates and grows, transforming itself into enriching experiences. On the other hand, negative thoughts act like weeds that can suffocate this natural growth process, limiting possibilities and creating barriers that hinder the blossoming of abundance. To cultivate a fertile mental field, it is crucial not only to select the thoughts we feed but also to be aware of how we perceive and reframe them.

Modern science, especially areas like quantum physics, reinforces the idea that reality is intimately connected to the observer. Just as simple observation can alter the behavior of subatomic particles, our thoughts have the capacity to impact the physical world and the circumstances around us. In this sense, by directing our minds towards positive frequencies, we create a vibration that resonates with what we wish to attract. Cultivating gratitude, practicing visualization, and maintaining a positive environment are concrete steps that strengthen this energy field, allowing abundance and well-being to flow naturally.

Positive thoughts are like seeds planted in fertile soil. They germinate, grow, and bear fruit, bringing positive experiences, opportunities, and enriching relationships into your life. When you cultivate optimism, hope, and gratitude, you are opening the doors for abundance to flow freely in all areas of your life.

The impact of thoughts on reality is a profound and transformative phenomenon. Quantum physics, by revealing that reality is a field of infinite possibilities, also shows us that the simple act of observing can influence the behavior of subatomic particles. This scientific finding resonates directly with the power of human thoughts. When you direct your mind towards positive thoughts, you raise your energy vibration and align yourself with the frequency of abundance. This vibrational state naturally attracts people, situations, and opportunities that reflect this same positive energy, creating a continuous cycle of prosperity and well-being.

On the other hand, negative thoughts — such as fear, doubt, and pessimism — diminish this vibration, building invisible barriers that impede the flow of abundance. It is as if you were erecting energetic walls that block opportunities and enriching experiences. This dense energy creates an internal environment that reinforces limitations and obstacles, making it more difficult to achieve desired goals. Therefore, understanding this mechanism is essential to take control of one's own reality and transform the way you interact with the world.

Transforming the mind into a true magnet for prosperity and optimism is a continuous process that requires practice, discipline, and patience. Just as strengthening a muscle requires regular exercise, the development of positive thoughts is consolidated with time and repetition. This gradual change not only alters your internal perspective but also directly influences your actions and the opportunities you attract. There are effective strategies that can be applied daily to cultivate a more optimistic and constructive mindset.

The first step on this journey is awareness. Becoming an observer of your own thoughts throughout the day is fundamental. Identifying patterns of negativity or self-sabotage allows you to question whether these thoughts are aligned with the results you want to achieve. For example, when noticing the recurrence of thoughts like "this will never work," it is important to recognize them without judgment and then reflect on their veracity. This simple act of observing and questioning is the starting point for initiating a mental transformation.

Next comes the reframing of these thoughts. This process consists of replacing negative ideas with more positive and empowering versions. It is not about denying life's challenges, but about facing them with a proactive and constructive mindset. For example, when faced with an obstacle, instead of thinking "I will never succeed," you can tell yourself: "I am learning and evolving with each step." This habit creates new neural pathways, making positive thinking more natural and automatic over time.

Another powerful resource is positive affirmations. These phrases, repeated regularly, have the ability to reprogram the subconscious mind. Choose affirmations that are aligned with your deepest goals and desires, and repeat them especially when the mind is most receptive, such as upon waking or before sleeping. Examples include: "I am capable of achieving my goals," "I attract prosperity in all areas of my life," or "I trust the natural flow of the universe." The constant repetition of these statements creates a solid foundation for self-confidence and motivation.

The practice of gratitude also plays an essential role in this process. Taking a few minutes of the day to reflect on everything you already have and value significantly changes your emotional vibration. Be grateful for your health, relationships, achievements, or even the small moments of everyday joy. Keeping a gratitude journal helps to consolidate this habit, directing focus to the positive and shifting attention away from what is lacking. This simple daily exercise strengthens the feeling of fullness and attracts even more reasons to be grateful.

Creative visualization is another powerful technique for shaping the desired reality. Imagine yourself fully experiencing the life you long for: with vibrant health, professional achievements, harmonious relationships, and financial prosperity. Visualize every detail clearly and engage emotionally in these scenes as if they were already part of your present. This practice not only strengthens motivation but also conditions the mind to seek paths and solutions that transform these dreams into reality.

In addition to these internal practices, the external environment exerts a great influence on mindset. Being surrounded by people who inspire, support, and encourage you is essential to maintain positivity. Healthy relationships and harmonious environments nurture the mind and spirit, reinforcing constructive mental patterns. Similarly, consuming positive content — such as self-help books, motivational lectures, and inspiring films — contributes to raising your energy.

It is equally important to be mindful of the information you consume. Negative news, toxic discussions, and content that feeds fear drain energy and undermine positivity. Replace these stimuli with sources that offer constructive knowledge and inspiration. This way, you create a lighter energy field that is more receptive to good opportunities.

Music and art are also powerful tools for influencing emotional state. Listening to music that uplifts the spirit, calms, or motivates has an immediate impact on energy vibration. Similarly, expressing yourself through art — whether writing, painting, dancing, or photographing — allows you to channel emotions in a creative and liberating way, further elevating your vibrational state.

Contact with nature is another valuable ally. Walking outdoors, feeling the breeze on your face, watching the sunrise or sunset, and listening to birdsong are simple but deeply restorative experiences. Nature has the ability to reconnect us with the present moment, dissolving tensions and renewing energy.

Finally, the regular practice of meditation is fundamental to cultivate inner peace and reduce stress. Meditation calms the mind, increases self-awareness, and creates space for positive thoughts to flourish. Start by dedicating a few minutes a day to this practice, focusing on your breath or guided meditations that encourage relaxation and optimism.

The benefits of cultivating positive thoughts are profound and encompass all areas of life. Stress and anxiety decrease, giving way to a sense of calm and balance. Physical health is strengthened, with improvements in the immune and cardiovascular systems. Creativity and problem-solving skills expand, allowing for innovative solutions to daily challenges. Relationships become more harmonious and enriching, and self-esteem grows, promoting confidence and self-reliance.

This transformation process does not happen overnight, but each step taken towards a more positive mindset builds a solid foundation for a fuller life. With discipline, practice, and patience, you will realize that the reality around you begins to mold itself according to the energy you cultivate internally.

Thus, by taking responsibility for your own thoughts and emotions, you become the architect of your own life. Each positive thought is a seed planted with intention and care, ready to bloom and transform your reality. This power to shape your own existence has always been in your hands — just choose to use it wisely and purposefully.

The transformation of our reality through positive thinking is a reflection of the inherent power of the human mind, a creative force that transcends mere observation. This phenomenon does not happen instantly or magically, but rather as a result of a continuous process of alignment between intention, belief, and action. Thus, true change begins in internal perception, where each thought planted with purpose and care creates roots that expand to influence external events. With this, our life becomes a genuine expression of the energy we cultivate.

When we accept the active role we play in constructing our experiences, we also assume the responsibility of choosing thoughts that promote growth and harmony. This inner work may seem challenging at first, but the fruits are undeniable. By focusing on constructive mental patterns, we create a natural flow of opportunities and synchronicities that confirm and reinforce the vibrations we emit. Each small adjustment in our mindset contributes to building a more coherent energy field aligned with our deepest desires.

The journey to a life of abundance does not depend solely on positive thoughts, but on a constant practice that integrates intention, action, and gratitude. By dedicating ourselves to this mental discipline, we realize that the changes we seek in the external world begin within ourselves. Over time, the synergy between our intentions and the events around us transforms the perception of our limitations into a horizon of infinite possibilities, ending the chapter with the certainty that the power to shape our reality is, and always has been, in our own hands.

Chapter 3
Powerful Affirmations

Words exert a direct and significant influence on the construction of personal reality. By consciously choosing positive and empowering statements, it is possible to direct the mind towards achieving goals and overcoming challenges. Affirmations are powerful tools that act as catalysts for internal change, creating a mental environment conducive to the development of self-confidence, motivation, and clarity of purpose. When incorporated with intention and consistency, they shape thoughts, behaviors, and emotions, promoting a profound and lasting transformation. This process involves replacing limiting beliefs with constructive ideas, capable of driving the achievement of goals and strengthening self-perception.

The constant practice of affirmations strengthens the neural connections responsible for positive habits and productive mental patterns. Each sentence affirmed with conviction acts as a seed that, cultivated with persistence, blossoms into attitudes consistent with the desired objectives. Thus, the conscious use of words becomes a powerful strategy to realign the mind and behavior, leading to concrete results in various areas of life. This transformation does not happen instantly, but gradually, through a continuous process of repetition, reflection, and living the affirmations, which solidifies new beliefs and behaviors aligned with personal growth.

Over time, affirmations cease to be mere words and become part of the identity of those who practice them, positively influencing decisions, relationships, and opportunities. The mind adapts to new ideas and begins to operate in a more assertive and optimistic way, paving the way for a more balanced, abundant, and meaningful life. This daily commitment to positive thoughts not only strengthens resilience in the face of challenges, but also creates a virtuous cycle of self-confidence, focus, and achievement. Thus, adopting powerful affirmations as part of your routine is a fundamental step to achieve a complete and sustainable transformation.

Imagine your mind as a garden. If you plant weed seeds, they will grow and suffocate the flowers. Similarly, if you feed your mind with negative thoughts and limiting beliefs, they will take root and block the flow of abundance. Affirmations are like seeds of vibrant and fragrant flowers that, when planted and cultivated with care, transform your mental garden into an oasis of positivity and prosperity.

The subconscious mind functions as a vast program that regulates thoughts, emotions, and behaviors, directly influencing how we experience reality. Responsible for a large part of the automatic decisions we make, it stores deep-seated beliefs that guide our daily actions. Powerful affirmations act precisely at this hidden level, reprogramming limiting patterns and replacing them with positive and empowering thoughts. This process is similar to updating an internal operating system: each word affirmed with conviction installs new ideas, gradually shaping the perception we have of ourselves and the world.

By repeating affirmations charged with intention and emotion, we create new neural connections. This reinforces positive mental pathways that influence attitudes, decisions, and even the way we face challenges. This repetition is not just a formality, but a practice that, over time, transforms negative beliefs into self-confidence and motivation. The mind begins to operate at a higher frequency, attuned to goals of growth, overcoming, and achievement.

For affirmations to be truly effective, their formulation must follow some fundamental principles. First, they need to be positive. The mind does not process negations well, so phrases like "I don't want to fail anymore" are less effective than "I am capable of achieving my goals." By stating what you want to achieve, you direct your energy towards concrete and constructive results.

Constructing affirmations in the present tense is equally important. Saying "I will be successful" projects the desire into an indefinite future, while "I am successful" creates an immediate connection with this reality, causing the brain to recognize this state as something already existing. This simple detail reinforces the idea that change is already underway.

Specificity is another essential pillar. Vague affirmations tend to have limited impact because they do not offer a clear focus for the subconscious mind. By detailing exactly what you want, you facilitate the visualization and realization of your goals. For example, stating "I prosper financially with my creative work" is more powerful than simply saying "I want to be rich."

The use of the first person strengthens the connection with the affirmation. Phrases that begin with "I am" or "I have" create a direct link between what is affirmed and who you are. This reinforces personal responsibility for one's own transformation and increases the authenticity of the statement. This personal bond awakens commitment to the process of change.

Furthermore, charging affirmations with intense emotion enhances their effects. Genuinely feeling what you are affirming — joy, gratitude, or enthusiasm — amplifies the connection between the conscious and subconscious mind. This emotional involvement causes the mind to register the affirmation as something real and urgent, accelerating its manifestation.

Practical examples of powerful affirmations can be incorporated to work on various areas of life. In the field of prosperity, for example, stating "I am a magnet for prosperity and abundance. Money flows to me with ease and joy" activates an abundance mindset and opens space for financial opportunities. For health, the phrase "My body is healthy, strong, and full of vitality. I take care of myself with love and respect" strengthens the commitment to self-care and physical well-being.

Relationships can also be nurtured by affirmations such as "I attract loving and healthy relationships. I am loved and valued for who I am." This phrase reinforces self-worth and the belief that positive emotional connections are possible and deserved. In the field of self-esteem, statements like "I love and accept myself completely. I am worthy of love, happiness, and success" help to build a solid foundation of self-worth and confidence.

To effectively apply these affirmations in everyday life, some simple habits can be incorporated. Choosing affirmations aligned with your real goals is the first step. There is no point in repeating phrases that do not resonate with your needs and desires. They need to have true meaning and represent genuine aspirations.

Consistent repetition is also essential. Setting aside specific times of the day, such as upon waking and before bed, to affirm your statements reinforces the message in the subconscious mind. This habit creates a constant rhythm of mental reprogramming.

Writing down affirmations and keeping them close by is a powerful strategy. Writing phrases on cards and placing them in visible places — such as on the mirror, on the desk, or on the refrigerator door — serves as a constant reminder of what you are cultivating. This frequent visual contact reinforces the message and keeps the focus on the goals.

Detailed visualization further enhances the impact of affirmations. As you repeat each sentence, clearly imagine the realization of what is being affirmed. Involve all your senses in this visualization: feel, see, hear, and even imagine the scents or textures associated with your goal. This mental experience brings the desired reality closer.

Another effective practice is the use of mirrors. Looking directly into your own eyes while affirming your desires strengthens the connection with the subconscious and increases the credibility of the words. This daily exercise, although simple, has a profound impact on self-confidence.

Recording affirmations in your own voice and listening to them in moments of relaxation is also an excellent way to reinforce your inner messages. The familiarity of your own voice increases the authenticity of the affirmation and facilitates absorption by the subconscious.

Furthermore, creating a vision board with images, words, and symbols that represent your goals can be a powerful stimulus. Integrating affirmations into this board reinforces the emotional and mental connection with desires, making them more tangible.

Incorporating affirmations into meditation further amplifies their effects. In a state of deep relaxation, the subconscious is more receptive, facilitating the integration of new beliefs. Repeating affirmations during meditation creates an internal environment conducive to transformation.

This process of continuous and committed affirmation does not result in instant changes, but gradually builds a stronger, more resilient and confident mindset. Each repetition solidifies new beliefs and drives behaviors aligned with personal goals. The transformation occurs from the inside out, reflecting in the attitudes, decisions, and opportunities that arise.

By integrating powerful affirmations into your daily routine, you create a virtuous cycle of self-confidence, focus, and achievement. Each small victory reinforces the belief that larger goals are also achievable. With patience, dedication, and authenticity, this daily commitment translates into concrete and lasting results.

Thus, affirmations cease to be just words to become a reflection of the identity that is being built. They begin to guide thoughts, emotions, and behaviors, shaping a new reality, more abundant, balanced, and aligned with your true purposes. With each sentence affirmed with conviction, a seed of transformation is planted — and, with care and persistence, blossoms into real achievements.

Powerful affirmations are not just loose words, but instruments of profound transformation when aligned with genuine intention and constant practice. Incorporating them into everyday life is a process of self-knowledge and self-development that strengthens the mind and spirit. Over time, these positive statements come to reflect not only thoughts, but attitudes and behaviors that shape a new reality, more aligned with personal desires and purposes. It is in this continuous process of affirmation and action that true change occurs, solidifying a mindset of growth and fulfillment.

By allowing affirmations to become part of your routine, each small achievement reinforces the confidence that it is possible to achieve larger goals.

This positive cycle fuels motivation and creates a solid foundation to face challenges with resilience and clarity. The transformation happens gradually, but consistently, leading to a fuller, more balanced, and meaningful life. Affirmations cease to be mere words and become the reflection of a new identity, strengthened by beliefs that drive growth and overcoming.

Thus, cultivating powerful affirmations is a daily commitment to one's own well-being and success. The journey requires patience, dedication, and authenticity, but the return is immeasurable. Each sentence affirmed with conviction is a seed planted that, with care and persistence, blossoms into real achievements. This continuous process not only transforms the mind, but also opens doors to opportunities, connections, and experiences that reflect the abundance and balance sought.

Chapter 4
Creative Visualization

Creative visualization is an effective mental process that directs thoughts and emotions towards the achievement of goals and dreams. This practice involves constructing detailed mental images of desired situations, promoting a deep connection between mind and body. By creating clear and engaging scenes, the mind adapts to the new projected reality, awakening emotional and behavioral reactions that favor the achievement of objectives. This approach is not just an abstract technique, but a proven mechanism that directly influences behavior and decisions, increasing the chances of personal and professional success.

By cultivating mental images rich in detail and emotions, an alignment occurs between thoughts and actions, creating a mental state conducive to identifying opportunities and overcoming challenges. This process involves more than just thinking positively; it is about mentally incorporating each step necessary to achieve concrete results. The mind, when trained consistently, begins to recognize possible paths and develops a more confident and motivated posture. This internal alignment facilitates overcoming obstacles and promotes persistence in the face of difficulties.

With the regular practice of creative visualization, it is possible to establish a continuous cycle of motivation and action. The mental clarity generated allows decisions to be made with more assertiveness, while the emotional connection with the objective keeps focus and determination high. This harmonious integration between thought, emotion and behavior strengthens the ability to transform desires into reality, contributing to a more consistent and satisfying journey of personal growth.

Imagine an Olympic athlete preparing for a competition. He not only trains physically, but also visualizes every movement, every stage of the race, feeling the emotion of victory even before entering the track. In the same way, creative visualization allows you to "train" your mind for success, creating a detailed mental map of the path that will lead you to the realization of your dreams.

The power of creative visualization lies in the ability to transform thoughts into reality. When you vividly imagine your goals being achieved, your mind reacts as if it were actually living that experience. This phenomenon occurs because the brain does not distinguish what is real from what is intensely imagined. Thus, by creating clear and emotionally charged mental images, you trigger neurological and physiological processes that align your thoughts, emotions and behaviors with your goals. This alignment creates a mental path that directs your actions and decisions, making the realization of your desires something tangible.

On a mental level, visualization helps to build a detailed internal roadmap, organizing ideas and strategies. This allows for more assertive decision-making and the ability to see opportunities that were previously overlooked. The mental clarity obtained with this practice eliminates doubts and reinforces focus, facilitating overcoming obstacles and persistence in the face of challenges. Visualizing is not just imagining a final result, but also integrating each step necessary to achieve it.

In the emotional field, creative visualization awakens positive feelings such as enthusiasm, joy and gratitude. These emotions are fundamental to maintaining high motivation, as they reinforce confidence in one's own abilities and maintain enthusiasm throughout the journey. When you feel as if you have already achieved your goal, the emotion generated intensifies the commitment to your goals and accelerates the manifestation process.

Physically, the body also responds to the mental images created. Visualizing positive situations stimulates the release of well-being hormones, such as endorphins, dopamine and serotonin. These neurotransmitters promote relaxation, reduce stress and increase physical disposition, preparing the body to act with energy and resistance. The body, in harmony with the mind, becomes a more efficient instrument for achieving goals.

On the energy level, visualization adjusts the vibrational frequency of your personal energy. When you tune in to the vibration of what you want to attract, your energy aligns with the opportunities and circumstances necessary to achieve your goals. This vibrational state facilitates connection with people, situations and resources that contribute to the realization of your dreams, creating synchronicities and opening new paths.

For creative visualization to be effective, it is essential that it be done with vivid details. Imagine every aspect of the desired scene clearly, involving all the senses. Visualize the colors, smell the aromas, hear the sounds and perceive the textures. The more realistic this mental image is, the deeper the impact on the subconscious. This richness of detail transforms visualization into a complete experience, reinforcing the commitment to achieving the goal.

In addition to details, emotional intensity is crucial. Connect deeply with the positive emotions that accompany achieving your goal. Feel the joy, relief, satisfaction and pride as if everything were already happening. These emotions not only intensify the experience, but also enhance the impact of visualization, accelerating the realization process.

Keeping the focus exclusively on what you want to achieve is another essential element. Replace thoughts of doubt or fear with positive and inspiring images. Directing your attention to the desired results helps to keep the mind aligned with your goals, preventing distractions that can undermine confidence.

It is important that the visualized goals are ambitious, but achievable. Visualizing realistic yet challenging goals creates a balance between inspiration and credibility. This balance increases motivation and avoids frustration, maintaining enthusiasm and persistence.

Constant practice is the key to strengthening visualization. Make this exercise a daily habit. Take a few minutes each day to visualize your goals with intensity. The more times you repeat this process, the stronger and clearer the mental image will be, reinforcing your connection to what you want to manifest.

To start the practice of creative visualization, follow a simple and effective step-by-step. Start by clearly defining what you want to achieve. The more specific your goal, the easier it will be to build a vivid mental picture. Then choose a quiet environment where you can concentrate without interruption. Close your eyes, breathe deeply and allow yourself to relax, leaving your body light and your mind calm.

With a calm mind, start building the desired scene with a wealth of detail. Imagine yourself fully experiencing the achievement of your goal. Visualize the colors, sounds, smells and physical sensations of this experience. Feel the positive emotions associated with this achievement. Experience anticipatory gratitude, as if you were already enjoying what you are visualizing. This feeling raises your energy vibration and strengthens the belief that the goal is already part of your reality.

Practice this visualization daily. Set aside specific times of your day, such as when you wake up or before bed, to reinforce the mental image. Continuous repetition deepens the impact on the subconscious and keeps the focus firmly on your goals.

Some examples of visualizations can help guide your practice. To attract prosperity, imagine yourself receiving a significant amount of money. Feel the joy, gratitude and security that this financial abundance provides. Visualize yourself using this resource to make dreams come true and help other people. For health, imagine your body full of energy, light and healthy. Feel the vitality pulsating in each cell, perceive the freedom to move with ease and enjoy physical well-being.

In relationships, visualize yourself surrounded by loving, respectful people who share happy moments with you. Feel the affection, emotional connection and complicity flowing naturally. For your career, imagine yourself occupying your dream job, being recognized for your talent and dedication. Feel the satisfaction of doing meaningful work and the enthusiasm for growing professionally.

To enhance visualization, use complementary tools. Create a vision board with images, words and symbols that represent your goals. Place this board in a visible location to reinforce your intentions daily. Associate positive affirmations with your visualization, confidently declaring that your achievements are already real. Listen to music that evokes positive emotions and inspires connection with your goals. Practice visualization before bed, when the subconscious mind is most receptive.

Creative visualization, when incorporated consistently, becomes a powerful tool for transformation. It not only directs the mind towards clear goals, but also reprograms limiting beliefs, replacing them with empowering thoughts. By persisting in this practice, you align your desires with your actions, creating a solid foundation for achieving goals. The combination of vivid imagination and consistent action strengthens discipline, maintains motivation and opens paths to concrete results.

Over time, creative visualization promotes a profound inner transformation. Every thought visualized with clarity and emotion becomes a firm step towards your goals. Cultivating this habit brings you closer to fulfilling your dreams and reveals your unlimited potential, leading to a fuller, more abundant and fulfilling life.

Creative visualization, when consistently incorporated into everyday life, becomes a powerful tool for self-development. This process not only directs the mind towards specific goals, but also reconfigures limiting beliefs, replacing them with empowering thoughts. By persisting in this practice, the mind begins to operate in tune with the deepest intentions, creating a solid foundation for coherent and effective actions. This continuous connection between intention and behavior increases self-confidence and feeds a positive cycle of progressive achievements.

Furthermore, creative visualization can be integrated with other personal development practices, such as meditation, goal writing and setting measurable goals. This combination enhances the effects of visualization, allowing each mental image to gain more strength and clarity. Thus, the person not only dreams, but also structures concrete ways to transform those dreams into reality. This balance between imagination and action strengthens discipline and keeps motivation high, even in the face of unexpected challenges.

Over time, the constant practice of creative visualization promotes a profound inner transformation, aligning desires with behaviors and creating previously invisible opportunities. Every thought visualized with clarity and emotion becomes a firm step towards the goals set. In this way, cultivating this habit not only brings you closer to fulfilling your dreams, but also awakens a new perception of your unlimited potential, leading to a fuller and more fulfilling life.

Chapter 5
The Law of Attraction

    The Law of Attraction operates continuously and directly in all aspects of life, influencing the reality of each individual according to their thoughts, emotions, and beliefs. By recognizing that everything in the universe is energy in motion, it becomes evident that every idea and feeling that manifests within us carries a vibration capable of interacting with the surrounding environment. This constant interaction shapes daily experiences, attracting situations and opportunities that reflect the predominant energy pattern. Thus, cultivating positive thoughts, elevated feelings, and empowering beliefs is not just a mental exercise, but a concrete way to direct one's life towards more harmonious and prosperous paths.

    Deeply understanding this principle allows for a shift in perspective, where each individual becomes responsible for co-creating their reality consciously. This means that by aligning clear intentions with consistent actions, it is possible to transform desires into tangible experiences. From this understanding, the opportunity arises to use personal power to attract prosperity, health, love, and achievements in various areas. This process requires not only changing thoughts but also cultivating positive emotions and eliminating limiting beliefs that may block the natural flow of abundance.

By assuming an active role in creating one's own reality, each choice becomes a powerful tool to manifest desired outcomes. Developing the habit of focusing attention on what is desired, maintaining a high vibration through gratitude, visualization, and aligned actions, establishes a direct connection with the right opportunities. In this way, life becomes a reflection of conscious intentions, allowing one to experience experiences that truly correspond to the deepest desires, creating a continuous cycle of growth, fulfillment, and plenitude.

Imagine the universe as a vast ocean of energy, where each drop vibrates at a specific frequency. Your thoughts and emotions are like waves that propagate in this ocean, attracting other waves of similar frequency. If you emanate vibrations of joy, gratitude, and prosperity, you will attract experiences that resonate with that same frequency, creating a virtuous cycle of abundance.

The Law of Attraction is a universal force that acts continuously, shaping the reality of each individual according to their thoughts, emotions, and beliefs. Everything in the universe is composed of energy in constant motion, and this energy responds directly to the vibration we emit. Each thought and emotion functions as a frequency that propagates and interacts with the environment around us, attracting circumstances, people, and opportunities that vibrate in the same tune.

Thus, by cultivating positive thoughts, elevated emotions, and empowering beliefs, we are, in practice, directing our lives towards more prosperous and harmonious paths.

Understanding this principle transforms the way we view our experiences. We cease to be victims of chance and assume the role of co-creators of our reality. This understanding reveals that thoughts and emotions are not just fleeting internal states, but creative forces that shape what we experience. When we align our desires with consistent actions and positive emotions, we connect directly with the natural flow of abundance. This process requires vigilance over limiting beliefs that may block this flow and the willingness to replace them with ideas that favor growth.

Taking control of one's own reality is a powerful choice. Every decision, however small it may seem, is a seed planted in the fertile ground of the mind. Focusing attention on what is desired, maintaining a high vibration through gratitude, visualization, and aligned actions, creates an energetic connection with the opportunities that favor the fulfillment of these desires. Thus, life becomes a reflection of the intentions we choose to nurture, creating a continuous cycle of growth and fulfillment.

Imagine the universe as an immense vibrational field, where everything is interconnected by energy frequencies. Our thoughts and emotions are waves that propagate in this field, attracting to us everything that vibrates in a similar way. If we emanate feelings of joy, gratitude, and love, we tune in to positive experiences and opportunities that reinforce these states. Likewise, if we maintain thoughts of fear or scarcity, we attract situations that reflect these vibrations.

To apply the Law of Attraction effectively, it is essential to understand its fundamental principles. The first of these is that everything is energy. Every thought, emotion, and belief we hold is a form of energy that interacts with the universe. When we realize that our ideas have creative power, we can consciously choose thoughts that are aligned with the outcomes we wish to manifest.

The second principle is that like attracts like. The energy you emit acts like a magnet, attracting circumstances that are on the same frequency. Positive thoughts and elevated emotions create an energy field conducive to the manifestation of positive experiences. On the other hand, negative thoughts attract challenges and obstacles. Therefore, cultivating a positive mindset is essential to attract a prosperous reality.

Another central aspect is recognizing that you are a co-creator of your reality. Every choice, thought, and feeling directly influences what you experience. By acting with awareness and intention, you take control of the flow of energy that shapes your life. This means that the responsibility for the results is in your hands, but also the power to transform any situation.

The vibration and frequency with which you operate are decisive. Practices such as meditation, gratitude, and creative visualization help to raise your vibration, aligning your energy with the frequency of abundance. The more you maintain this high vibration, the easier it will be to attract positive experiences.

Focus and attention are powerful tools. Where you focus your attention, your energy flows. If you dedicate your focus to your goals with clarity and consistency, you create an energy field that facilitates the fulfillment of these desires. Distractions or scattered thoughts weaken this field, while directed attention strengthens it.

To put these principles into practice, start by clearly defining what you want. Clarity of intention is essential to channel your energy effectively. Be specific and detailed in your goals. Visualize your desires with rich details, imagine yourself living this reality and get emotionally involved with this experience. Feel the joy, gratitude, and satisfaction of having already achieved what you desire.

Positive affirmations are valuable tools to reprogram the subconscious mind. Declare with conviction phrases that reinforce your goals, such as "I am worthy of prosperity and success" or "I am open to receiving love and abundance in my life." The daily repetition of these affirmations strengthens the belief that your desires are possible and close to being fulfilled.

Action is an indispensable component of the Law of Attraction. Thinking and feeling positively are fundamental, but it is through consistent and intentional actions that opportunities materialize. Move towards your dreams, make decisions aligned with your goals, and take advantage of opportunities that arise.

Gratitude is a practice that amplifies positive vibration. Give thanks for all that you already have and for what is on its way. This state of appreciation raises your energy frequency, opening space to receive even more. Gratitude transforms the perception of reality, making it lighter and more abundant.

Release internal resistance. Limiting beliefs, fears, and doubts block the flow of abundance. Identify these blockages and work to dissolve them, whether through self-knowledge, therapies, or techniques such as Ho'oponopono. By releasing these barriers, you allow energy to flow freely, facilitating the manifestation of your desires.

Trust the process. Develop the confidence that the universe is conspiring in your favor. Results do not always appear immediately, but maintaining faith and patience is essential. This full trust keeps your vibration high and strengthens your connection with the natural flow of life.

To exemplify the practical application of the Law of Attraction, think of manifesting prosperity. Visualize yourself receiving money with ease, paying your bills with peace of mind, and investing in personal projects. Feel the security and financial freedom. At the same time, adopt habits that support this abundance mindset, such as financial planning and developing new skills.

In the field of relationships, imagine yourself sharing happy moments with a loving and respectful partner. Feel loved and valued. At the same time, develop self-love, participate in social settings, and be open to new connections. This balance between desire and action creates the ideal environment to attract a healthy relationship.

For health, visualize yourself with energy and vitality. Feel your body light and balanced. Adopt healthy habits such as a balanced diet, physical exercise, and relaxation practices. This commitment to well-being strengthens your vibration and attracts full health.

By integrating these principles into your daily life, subtle changes begin to occur. Coincidences, opportunities, and meaningful encounters arise as reflections of your energetic alignment. With each achievement, your confidence in the power of the mind and emotions is strengthened, encouraging the continuity of this practice.

Over time, the Law of Attraction becomes more than a technique - it integrates into your way of being. Obstacles are seen as learning experiences, and life flows more lightly and abundantly. This continuous process of self-knowledge and conscious action reveals the unlimited potential of each person to create a full and meaningful reality. By taking responsibility for your own life, you discover that true transformation begins within you, and that the universe responds to every thought, emotion, and action with infinite possibilities.

By integrating these principles into everyday life, it is possible to perceive subtle but profound changes in daily experiences. Small signs, coincidences, and opportunities begin to appear, confirming that the energy alignment is in harmony with the cultivated desires. This process reinforces confidence in the power of the mind and emotions, encouraging a constant practice of positive thoughts and conscious actions. With each achievement, however modest, the understanding that we are co-authors of our own history is consolidated, guiding it with intention and purpose.

Over time, this new pattern of thinking becomes natural, transforming challenges into opportunities for growth and learning. Obstacles that once seemed insurmountable are now seen as stepping stones to personal evolution. This positive outlook does not deny the existence of difficulties, but allows them to be faced with resilience and wisdom, trusting that each experience contributes to the development and fulfillment of dreams. Thus, the Law of Attraction is revealed not only as a tool for conquest, but as a path of self-knowledge and expansion of consciousness.

Therefore, embracing responsibility for your own reality is also an invitation to inner transformation. By cultivating thoughts and feelings aligned with your desires, acting with determination, and maintaining faith in the process, you create the ideal conditions for life to flow more lightly and abundantly. This path of conscious manifestation leads not only to the achievement of goals, but also to a fuller, more balanced existence in tune with the universe.

Chapter 6
Eliminating Limiting Beliefs

Limiting beliefs represent deep mental barriers that directly influence thoughts, behaviors, and decisions, restricting the potential for growth and prosperity. They are negative thought patterns, often rooted in childhood or acquired through past experiences and external influences, that shape the way a person perceives themselves, the world, and their possibilities. These self-sabotaging ideas hinder the achievement of goals and prevent full development, creating a constant feeling of incapacity and limitation. Recognizing the existence of these beliefs is the first fundamental step to transforming the mindset and opening the way to a more abundant and fulfilling life.

Overcoming these beliefs requires a conscious and strategic approach. It is essential to carefully observe recurring thoughts, behavior patterns, and emotional reactions to challenges and opportunities. Critical analysis of these aspects allows you to identify which ideas are limiting personal and professional progress. Questioning the veracity of these beliefs, confronting them with positive experiences and concrete evidence, facilitates the deconstruction of distorted concepts. From this process, it is possible to replace negative thoughts with positive and constructive affirmations that reinforce self-confidence and encourage the pursuit of new achievements. This change in perspective is essential to break free from internal limitations and open space for growth.

Adopting practices that help in mental reprogramming, such as daily affirmations, visualizations, and self-knowledge techniques, strengthens the ability to reframe limiting beliefs. Methods such as Neuro-Linguistic Programming (NLP), Ho'oponopono, and Emotional Freedom Techniques (EFT) are effective tools to modify mental and emotional patterns, promoting a more positive mindset that is open to opportunities. In addition, seeking professional support, such as therapy or coaching, can deepen the process of self-knowledge and accelerate the overcoming of these barriers. By integrating these strategies, it is possible to develop a mindset aligned with success, allowing abundance to flow freely and goals to be achieved with more ease and confidence.

Imagine a bird trapped in a cage. Its wings are strong, ready to fly great distances, but the limits of its prison prevent it from exploring the open sky. This is how limiting beliefs work: they are invisible bars that restrict the ability to achieve dreams and live fully. Although the potential for success and fulfillment is present, these mental barriers keep the person trapped in self-sabotaging behavior patterns, preventing them from taking higher flights.

To break these barriers, the first step is to identify the limiting beliefs that act silently in the mind. They usually operate subtly, as recurring and automatic thoughts. Phrases like "I'm not good enough", "I don't deserve to be happy" or "Money only brings problems" are clear signs that distorted ideas are shaping the perception of one's own ability and blocking opportunities. Observing the inner dialogue is essential to perceive these patterns. When negative thoughts arise, question: "Where does this idea come from?" and "Is it really true?" This process of reflection is the first step to weakening the power of these beliefs.

In addition to thoughts, fears and insecurities also reveal limiting beliefs. The fear of failure, rejection, or even success may be rooted in past experiences that have created a distorted view of one's own ability. By identifying these fears and understanding their origin, it is possible to begin to deconstruct them. For example, the fear of taking on great responsibilities may have arisen from constant criticism during childhood. Recognizing this origin allows you to reassess and reformulate these feelings.

Another indicator of limiting beliefs is repetitive behavior patterns. If you tend to give up on important projects, procrastinate, or self-sabotage when you are about to achieve something significant, these behaviors may be a direct result of unconscious beliefs. Analyzing these attitudes helps to understand how these ideas are influencing your decisions and how to break this harmful cycle.

Emotional reactions are also important clues. Frequent feelings of anxiety, frustration, or anger in the face of challenges can signal hidden limiting beliefs.

These emotional states serve as an alert that something needs to be adjusted internally. By welcoming these emotions and seeking to understand them, space is opened to transform them into more positive and constructive feelings.

The origin of these beliefs often goes back to childhood experiences. Phrases said by parents, teachers, or caregivers, such as "You will never be successful" or "Money doesn't grow on trees", can become deeply fixed in the subconscious. These negative messages, repeated over time, shape the way the person perceives themselves and relates to success and prosperity.

Traumatic experiences, such as family bankruptcies or financial losses, also leave marks that feed the idea that prosperity is not safe or possible. Similarly, the influence of the social environment, media, and culture reinforces beliefs of scarcity. Comments like "Money changes people" or "Rich people are bad" are internalized and make it difficult to accept abundance.

Social pressure and constant comparison with others are other factors that feed limiting beliefs. Social networks and standards imposed by society create a sense of inadequacy, leading to thoughts like "I'll never be good enough" or "I don't have what it takes to achieve success." Identifying these triggers is essential to break free from these comparisons and focus on personal development.

To eliminate limiting beliefs, it is necessary to adopt techniques that help in mental reprogramming.

The first step is to question these beliefs. Ask yourself: "Is this belief based on facts or distorted perceptions?" and "Is there any concrete evidence to prove this?" Revisiting times when you have overcome similar challenges can help weaken the strength of these ideas.

Another effective technique is reframing. Replace limiting thoughts with positive affirmations. If you tend to think "I'm not good enough", turn that thought into "I have unique skills and I'm constantly evolving". This new pattern of thinking, repeated frequently, reprograms the mind to see challenges as opportunities for growth.

Positive affirmations are fundamental in this process. Declare empowering phrases such as "I am worthy of prosperity and success" or "I have all the skills necessary to achieve my goals." Repeating these affirmations with emotion, especially upon waking and before bed, reinforces self-confidence and restructures subconscious beliefs.

Creative visualization is also a powerful tool. Imagine yourself fully experiencing your goals, with vivid details. Visualize yourself overcoming challenges with confidence, celebrating achievements, and living the reality you desire. The more real and engaging this practice is, the more the subconscious will accept this new reality as possible.

Techniques such as EFT (Emotional Freedom Techniques) are effective in releasing emotional blocks. By stimulating specific points on the body with light touches while verbalizing acceptance phrases, such as "Even though I am afraid of failing, I accept and love myself deeply", you dissolve negative emotional patterns and allow new positive beliefs to be incorporated.

Ho'oponopono is another transformative practice. Repeating the phrases "I'm sorry, please forgive me, I love you, I'm grateful" helps to clear painful memories and limiting beliefs, promoting inner peace and emotional balance. This process of reconciliation with the past frees up space for new thoughts and experiences.

Neuro-Linguistic Programming (NLP) and hypnosis are also advanced methods for reprogramming the subconscious. NLP works on the way you interpret your experiences, allowing you to modify negative thought patterns. Hypnosis, in turn, accesses deep states of the mind, facilitating the installation of new positive thoughts and behaviors.

Seeking professional support, such as therapy or coaching, can accelerate this process. A qualified therapist can help identify deep-seated limiting beliefs and guide the emotional healing process, while a coach can guide you in building new habits and strategies to achieve goals.

Finally, creating an environment that fosters personal growth is essential. Surround yourself with people who share positive thoughts and encourage development. Consume inspiring content, participate in self-knowledge events, and get involved in communities that value personal growth.

The transformation of limiting beliefs does not happen instantly, but through a continuous process of self-knowledge, practice, and persistence. With each new positive belief incorporated, the mind is strengthened, and the path to success and prosperity becomes clearer.

Taking control of one's own thoughts is an act of courage and freedom. By replacing self-sabotaging beliefs with empowering ideas, you expand your potential and create opportunities for a fuller and more abundant life. Each small step taken in this direction reinforces your ability to overcome challenges and build a reality aligned with your dreams.

To consolidate the transformation of the mind and definitively eliminate limiting beliefs, it is crucial to maintain consistency in the practices adopted. Mindset change does not occur instantly, but rather through a continuous process of self-knowledge and self-development. Cultivating daily habits that reinforce positive thoughts and actions aligned with your goals strengthens resilience and expands the ability to face challenges. This daily commitment creates a solid foundation to sustain personal and financial growth, allowing new empowering beliefs to take deep root.

In addition, surrounding yourself with environments and people that stimulate growth is fundamental to sustain this evolution. Participating in support groups, personal development events, or even consuming inspiring content can accelerate the change process. Living with individuals who share values of prosperity and overcoming fuels motivation and encourages persistence in the face of obstacles. Thus, the positive influence of the external environment acts as a powerful reinforcement in building an abundant mindset.

By integrating these new habits and perspectives into your routine, you take control of your own narrative, paving the way to achieve your dreams with confidence and determination. The limitations imposed by old beliefs lose strength in the face of a strengthened mindset, and the horizon of possibilities expands. With dedication and perseverance, each step taken represents a step towards a fuller, more prosperous life, aligned with the true potential that lies within you.

Chapter 7
Deep Self-Knowledge

Self-knowledge is an essential and transformative journey that allows you to deeply understand who you are, recognizing your beliefs, values, emotions, talents, and life purpose. By exploring each aspect of your being, you connect with your essence, identify behavior patterns, and discover hidden potentials. This inner dive provides clarity about your motivations and choices, allowing you to act with more awareness and authenticity. When you understand your limitations and strengths, you become capable of overcoming obstacles and directing your actions strategically, creating a solid path to achieve your goals and manifest the life you desire.

This process of self-discovery reveals not only skills and talents but also limiting beliefs and self-sabotaging behaviors that can hinder your growth. By recognizing these patterns, you develop the ability to transform them, replacing negative thoughts with more constructive and positive perspectives. This internal movement favors the creation of healthier habits, strengthens self-esteem, and broadens your vision of what is possible to achieve. Thus, self-knowledge becomes a powerful tool to align your actions with your values and purposes, facilitating the construction of a full and satisfying life.

Furthermore, deepening the knowledge about yourself directly impacts your relationships and decisions. You begin to act with more empathy and understanding, establishing more authentic and balanced connections. This connection with yourself generates inner peace, resilience, and security to face challenges and embrace opportunities. By developing this awareness, you unlock the natural flow of abundance in all areas of your life, living in a way that is more aligned with who you truly are and the paths you wish to follow.

Imagine yourself as an explorer venturing into a dense and unknown forest. Without a map or compass, each step is uncertain and full of hidden challenges. However, with the right tools, you begin to unravel trails, overcome obstacles, and eventually discover hidden treasures. Self-knowledge works exactly like this map: it illuminates paths, reveals pitfalls, and points to safe directions. When you dedicate yourself to understanding who you really are, you begin to navigate with more clarity through the complexity of your mind and emotions, unlocking the potential to achieve your dreams.

This inner dive is not just a process of self-analysis, but a profound journey that reveals beliefs, emotions, talents, and purposes. It provides clarity about your desires and choices, allowing you to act more consciously and authentically. By understanding your limitations and recognizing your strengths, you become able to overcome obstacles and direct your actions strategically. This inner alignment builds a solid foundation to achieve goals and manifest the life you desire.

More than identifying skills, self-knowledge brings to light behavior patterns and limiting beliefs that block growth. Recognizing these blocks allows you to replace them with constructive thoughts and positive habits. This inner transformation strengthens self-esteem, broadens the vision of what is possible to achieve, and aligns your actions with your deepest values. Thus, you pave the way for a full and satisfying life, where each decision is made with awareness and purpose.

By deepening the knowledge about yourself, your relationships and decisions are also transformed. With more empathy and understanding, you begin to establish authentic and balanced connections. This inner harmony generates peace, resilience, and security to face challenges and embrace opportunities. The connection with yourself unlocks the flow of abundance in all areas of life, allowing you to live aligned with your essence and walk confidently towards your goals.

Self-knowledge is essential to attract abundance because it reveals limiting beliefs that operate silently and block your potential. By identifying these patterns, you can replace them with empowering thoughts, creating a mindset conducive to growth. This process also allows you to recognize repetitive behaviors that hinder your progress. When you understand these cycles, it becomes possible to interrupt them and adopt new, more productive habits.

Furthermore, self-knowledge awakens talents and abilities that often remain dormant. By valuing these natural skills, you can direct your energy towards activities that generate satisfaction and fulfillment. This alignment with your potential abilities enhances your productivity and creativity, contributing to a more balanced and prosperous life.

Another transformative aspect of self-knowledge is the discovery of life purpose. Understanding what truly makes sense to you brings clarity and motivation, guiding your choices and actions. This alignment not only provides personal and professional fulfillment but also attracts opportunities consistent with your values.

Self-esteem is also strengthened throughout this journey. By accepting your qualities and recognizing aspects that need to be developed, you build a healthier relationship with yourself. This self-compassion increases self-confidence, allowing you to face challenges with more courage and determination.

In relationships, self-knowledge enhances the way you express yourself and connect with others. Understanding your emotions and reactions makes interactions more authentic and empathetic. This strengthens bonds and creates environments of respect and mutual understanding.

This process also promotes inner peace. By connecting with your deepest emotions and thoughts, you develop balance and harmony. This inner state facilitates the flow of abundance, as you begin to act with confidence, clarity, and purpose.

To deepen self-knowledge, some tools can be extremely effective. Introspection is one of them. Setting aside moments of silence to observe your thoughts and emotions, without judgment, allows you to identify patterns that influence your choices. This daily exercise strengthens self-awareness and helps you better deal with challenges.

Another powerful tool is journaling. Writing about your experiences, feelings, and reflections helps organize ideas and identify behavior patterns. This practice facilitates the release of repressed emotions and promotes mental clarity.

Meditation also plays a fundamental role. It calms the mind, reduces stress, and increases awareness of your thoughts and emotions. This state of presence allows you to identify and transform limiting beliefs, creating space for new perspectives.

Practices such as yoga integrate body, mind, and spirit, promoting physical and emotional balance. Postures and breathing techniques unlock tensions, favoring a deeper connection with yourself.

Reading books on personal development, spirituality, and psychology broadens your worldview and offers valuable tools for self-transformation. This habit stimulates critical reflection and inspires positive changes.

Seeking sincere feedback from trusted people is also essential. Listening to external perceptions about your attitudes can reveal strengths and aspects to be improved, broadening your vision of yourself.

Therapy is a powerful resource for exploring emotions, traumas, and unconscious patterns. With the support of a professional, you can deepen self-knowledge, identify emotional blocks, and develop strategies to overcome them.

Personality tests, such as the MBTI and the Enneagram, are useful for understanding your characteristics, preferences, and behaviors. These tools help you direct your choices in a way that is more aligned with your talents and values.

Dream analysis is also a way to access deep aspects of the mind. Observing and interpreting the symbols and narratives of dreams can reveal repressed emotions and internal conflicts.

Finally, travel and new experiences broaden your perception and challenge your beliefs. Stepping out of your comfort zone stimulates adaptation and strengthens self-confidence.

Unraveling your inner map involves understanding your values, beliefs, emotions, talents, and purpose. Identifying your values allows you to align decisions with what truly matters to you. Exploring beliefs reveals thoughts that drive or limit your growth. Recognizing emotions develops emotional intelligence, improving your reactions and relationships. Valuing talents strengthens your positive impact on the world. Discovering your purpose gives meaning to your actions. Identifying strengths enhances your skills, while working on aspects to be developed promotes evolution.

This journey of self-knowledge requires patience and commitment. Each discovery, whether comfortable or challenging, is an opportunity for adjustment and growth. Celebrating each step strengthens the motivation to continue evolving.

Deeply understanding yourself is a gift you give yourself. This knowledge illuminates the path to personal fulfillment and allows you to contribute positively to the world. Living in alignment with your values, purposes, and talents inspires other people to also seek their essence. Thus, self-knowledge becomes a collective force for transformation.

Deep self-knowledge also requires patience and persistence. Like any growth process, it does not happen instantly, but develops gradually as you allow yourself to explore different aspects of yourself. With each discovery, be it comfortable or challenging, comes the opportunity to adjust your choices and behaviors. This path, sometimes winding, strengthens your ability to adapt and resilience, preparing you to deal with adversity with more security and confidence.

By integrating self-knowledge into your routine, you begin to recognize the importance of celebrating small achievements and personal advancements. Each step taken towards a deeper understanding of who you are contributes to strengthening your self-confidence and self-esteem. This constant recognition reinforces the motivation to continue evolving and adjusting your actions according to your values and goals. Thus, you create a positive cycle of development, in which each reflection and learning drives new achievements.

Finally, understanding yourself in depth is a gift you give yourself. This inner knowledge not only illuminates the path to personal fulfillment but also allows you to contribute more meaningfully to the world around you. By living in tune with your values, purposes, and talents, you inspire other people to also seek their own essence. In this way, self-knowledge is transformed into a collective force, capable of generating positive and lasting changes in society.

Chapter 8
Inner Healing

Inner healing is an essential path to freeing yourself from emotional blocks and achieving a full life of abundance and well-being. This process involves the identification and transformation of deeply rooted traumas, fears, and insecurities, allowing repressed emotions to be understood and integrated in a healthy way. Just as a river finds its natural flow when unblocked, the mind and heart harmonize when old wounds are healed, creating space for personal growth, prosperity, and emotional balance. This journey is an invitation to reconcile with your own past, promoting acceptance of who you are and openness to new possibilities.

When starting this healing process, it is essential to recognize that all lived experiences, including painful ones, have shaped who you have become. Each challenge faced has contributed to your development, and understanding this is the first step towards transformation. From this awareness, it becomes possible to release negative patterns and limiting beliefs that sabotage progress. Self-compassion plays a crucial role in this path, as it allows you to look at yourself with kindness, respecting the time needed to heal wounds and move forward with confidence. This self-care strengthens self-esteem and opens space for the manifestation of dreams and goals previously blocked by insecurities.

Adopting self-knowledge and self-care practices is essential to consolidate inner healing. Techniques such as meditation, therapeutic writing, and seeking professional support offer powerful tools for dealing with challenging emotions. Furthermore, cultivating healthy habits, such as regular physical exercise, a balanced diet, and leisure time, contributes to the balance between body and mind. Over time, this dedication to well-being promotes a feeling of lightness and freedom, allowing you to connect with your true essence and manifest a richer, more meaningful life aligned with your values.

Inner healing is like caring for a garden that has been neglected for a long time. Its roots may be suffocated by weeds of trauma, hurt, and limiting beliefs. However, with attention, care, and patience, this garden can flourish again. Likewise, when you decide to face your emotional wounds and release patterns that block your growth, you create space for a deep and true transformation. This process is not instantaneous, but a continuous journey of self-understanding, acceptance, and liberation.

Recognizing that past experiences, especially painful ones, have shaped who you are today is the first step to healing. Traumas, losses, and rejections leave deep marks that, when left untreated, continue to influence your decisions, your relationships, and your ability to thrive. These wounds can manifest in different ways: as limiting beliefs that restrict your actions, as self-sabotaging behaviors, or even as physical and emotional symptoms.

Limiting beliefs, often unconscious, function as invisible barriers that prevent the realization of dreams. Recurring thoughts such as "I'm not good enough" or "I don't deserve to be happy" take root in the subconscious and directly affect your choices. Questioning the origin of these beliefs and replacing them with positive and constructive thoughts is essential to free yourself from these bonds.

Self-destructive behaviors, such as procrastination, addictions, or involvement in toxic relationships, are also reflections of unhealed emotional wounds. These attitudes arise as unconscious defense mechanisms against pain, but end up hindering growth and evolution. Breaking these patterns requires courage, self-knowledge, and the adoption of healthy habits that promote well-being.

Furthermore, repressed emotions can manifest in the body, resulting in physical illnesses and emotional disorders such as anxiety, depression, and chronic pain. The body is a reflection of the internal emotional state, and ignoring these signs can aggravate suffering. Practices that promote emotional and physical balance are fundamental to dissolving these blocks.

Difficulties in manifesting desires and goals often stem from deep emotional blocks. Even with effort and dedication, the feeling of stagnation can persist. This is because negative beliefs and emotional patterns create resistance to the flow of abundance. Healing these wounds releases the energy necessary for thoughts, emotions, and actions to be in harmony, facilitating full realization.

Starting the inner healing process requires acknowledging and embracing your own pain. This is an act of courage and self-love. Instead of avoiding difficult emotions, allow yourself to feel and understand what they want to reveal. Writing about your experiences, practicing meditation, or talking to someone you trust are effective ways to access and process repressed emotions.

Seeking therapeutic support is a powerful tool on this journey. Trained professionals can help explore the roots of trauma and offer strategies to overcome it. Therapies such as cognitive behavioral therapy, Jungian analysis, and integrative therapies are resources that favor the understanding and reframing of painful experiences.

Emotional release techniques, such as EFT (Emotional Freedom Techniques), Ho'oponopono, and Family Constellation, are effective methods for accessing and dissolving deeply rooted negative emotions. These practices help to process repressed feelings and reframe experiences, promoting emotional lightness and mental clarity.

Meditation is a practice that strengthens the connection with yourself and calms the mind. It allows you to observe your own thoughts and emotions without judgment, creating space for self-compassion and acceptance. Mindfulness techniques, guided meditations, and creative visualizations are paths that relieve stress and unlock emotions.

Yoga is also a powerful healing tool. It integrates body, mind, and spirit, promoting balance and harmony. Conscious movements and controlled breathing help release physical and emotional tension, unlocking the body's vital energy. This practice strengthens inner connection and promotes discipline, focus, and serenity.

Forgiveness is one of the most important pillars of inner healing. Forgiving yourself and others does not mean justifying negative attitudes, but freeing yourself from the emotional weight that prevents you from moving forward. Reflection practices, forgiveness letters (even if they are not sent), and specific meditations help dissolve resentment, bringing peace and lightness.

Reconnecting with your inner child is an essential step. Many of the deepest emotional wounds originate in childhood. Embracing this part of yourself with love and compassion allows you to heal painful memories and recover joy, spontaneity, and creativity. Visualizing happy moments, writing letters to the child you were, or engaging in pleasurable activities are ways to strengthen this connection.

Releasing guilt and shame is another fundamental step. These heavy emotions paralyze and keep you trapped in the past. Accepting that mistakes are part of the learning process and that you did the best you could with the emotional resources you had at the time is essential. Forgiveness practices and positive affirmations help dissolve these feelings.

Self-compassion is a constant practice of kindness and understanding towards yourself. Replacing self-criticism with loving thoughts strengthens self-esteem and creates a safe inner environment to grow. Mindfulness, daily affirmations, and moments of self-care are practices that cultivate this healthy relationship with yourself.

Celebrating each achievement, no matter how small, reinforces the path of inner healing. Valuing daily progress, such as overcoming a fear or maintaining a healthy routine, strengthens self-confidence and creates a positive cycle of evolution. Keeping a gratitude journal, sharing victories, or rewarding yourself for goals achieved are ways to acknowledge your own progress.

This journey of inner healing requires patience, commitment, and courage. Each step, however small it may seem, contributes to the release of old patterns and the construction of a new reality. Transformation does not happen linearly, and moments of discomfort may arise, but it is precisely in these moments that resilience and self-compassion become essential.

As you progress on this path, you will notice subtle and profound changes in your life. Emotions flow more lightly, thoughts become more positive, and actions more aligned with your values. This inner balance is reflected in the outside world, opening doors to new opportunities and experiences that previously seemed unattainable.

By taking care of your inner garden, you allow abundance, joy, and peace to flourish. Inner healing is not just a process of overcoming, but a path of reconciliation with who you are. With a light heart and a clear mind, you become capable of living with more authenticity, freedom, and fullness.

This personal transformation not only impacts you, but also everyone around you. When you heal your wounds and live in harmony with yourself, you inspire other people to also seek their own process of healing and growth. Thus, inner healing expands and creates waves of positive change, contributing to a more balanced and compassionate world.

Allow yourself to live this journey with courage and kindness. By taking care of yourself with love and patience, you will discover that it is possible to flourish in all areas of life, becoming a stronger, lighter, and more authentic version of yourself.

With further deepening in the journey of inner healing, it becomes evident that true transformation requires a continuous commitment to self-knowledge and the constant practice of healthy habits. Each small change, when integrated with intention and awareness, strengthens the emotional and mental foundation, allowing you to free yourself from old patterns and embrace new perspectives. By recognizing your limits and celebrating your victories, even the most subtle ones, you build a solid path towards balance and personal fulfillment, creating an internal environment conducive to flourishing fully.

This healing process is not linear and may present challenges, but it is precisely in these moments that resilience and self-compassion prove to be essential. By facing difficulties with patience and courage, you develop an inner strength capable of sustaining deep and lasting changes. Allowing yourself to feel, learn, and grow with each experience expands your ability to deal with adversity, promoting a more harmonious relationship with yourself and the world around you.

By integrating these teachings into your daily routine, you will realize that inner healing is a constant movement of reconciliation and renewal. With a lighter heart and a clear mind, new opportunities arise naturally, reflecting the abundance that already exists within you. Thus, the healing journey becomes a path of authenticity, where each step taken is an expression of self-love, freedom, and complete fulfillment.

Chapter 9
Abundance Mindset

Adopting an abundance mindset means recognizing that the world is full of opportunities, resources, and possibilities for everyone. This thinking is not based on illusions or assumptions, but on a concrete understanding that there is room for growth, success, and happiness in various areas of life. When you position yourself with confidence in the face of circumstances, you realize that it is possible to achieve your goals without the need to compete or fear scarcity. This perspective strengthens self-confidence, encourages optimism, and allows you to value every achievement, big or small, as part of a continuous flow of prosperity.

With this expanded vision, it becomes natural to act with gratitude and generosity, recognizing that sharing resources, knowledge, and time does not diminish what you have, but enhances the positive return. The abundance mindset leads to a collaborative stance, where the success of others inspires and motivates, instead of provoking feelings of threat or comparison. This creates a favorable environment for personal and collective growth, in which healthy relationships and genuine opportunities flourish. By embracing this mindset, you learn to face challenges as opportunities for evolution and understand that the universe is in constant motion, ready to support those who believe in their own potential.

This path to abundance involves conscious actions, such as the continuous development of skills, the practice of gratitude, and trust in the natural flow of life. Every attitude taken in this direction strengthens the perception that resources are unlimited when one is willing to learn, adapt, and collaborate. Thus, abundance manifests itself not only in material aspects, but also in relationships, health, emotional well-being, and personal fulfillment, creating a balanced and fulfilling existence.

Imagine yourself entering a large hall illuminated by golden chandeliers, where long tables are elegantly arranged, laden with colorful dishes and sparkling drinks. The platters overflow with delicacies from all over the world, each exuding tempting aromas. Fresh fruits, freshly baked breads, fine cheeses, and delicately decorated desserts compose the scene. Guests circulate among the tables with sincere smiles, serving themselves generously, while sharing stories and laughter. In this environment, no one worries about taking more food or whether the best slice will be taken by someone else. Everyone is fully confident that there is more than enough for everyone, and that by sharing, the experience becomes even more enjoyable. This is the abundance mindset: a quiet confidence that there is space and resources for everyone to thrive.

Now, contrast this scenario with a dark and silent environment, where a small table carries a few dishes, almost empty. The guests look suspiciously at each other, fearing that if they don't act quickly, they will run out of food. Every movement is calculated, every gesture is defensive. This is the essence of the scarcity mindset - a limited and anxious view that resources are insufficient, forcing people to compete and protect what little they believe they have. This constant fear of losing or not achieving what they want prevents generosity and blocks opportunities for growth.

While the scarcity mindset distorts the perception of reality, creating the illusion that success belongs to a few and that any achievement of others diminishes one's own chances, the abundance mindset frees one from this cycle. It opens your eyes to the vastness of possibilities that the world offers. The success of another person ceases to be a threat and becomes a source of inspiration. Sincere gratitude arises for what one already has and the confidence that the universe is always ready to provide what is needed to make dreams come true. This shift in perspective transforms not only the way challenges are faced, but also the way one interacts with the world and the people around them.

Adopting this new mindset involves cultivating habits that reinforce this generous and expansive vision. The practice of gratitude, for example, becomes a powerful tool. When you take time to reflect on each achievement, however small, you create a solid foundation of contentment that expands the perception of abundance. This constant exercise of recognition reinforces the idea that life is already rich and full, allowing more prosperity to flow naturally.

Furthermore, acting with generosity becomes natural. Sharing is not limited to material goods, but involves time, knowledge, and emotional support. By offering help without expecting anything in return, one realizes that this genuine exchange generates mutual benefits. The positive energy returned fuels a continuous cycle of growth and well-being. The simple act of listening to someone attentively or offering a word of encouragement can be as valuable as any material gift.

Maintaining optimism in the face of adversity is another fundamental characteristic of this mindset. Obstacles are no longer seen as insurmountable barriers and are seen as valuable lessons. This hopeful outlook makes every challenge an opportunity for learning. Confidence in one's own abilities is reinforced, allowing one to face difficult situations with courage and determination. Self-confidence is solidified by realizing that every step taken, even in the face of difficulties, brings you closer to your goals.

The power of collaboration also stands out. Understanding that working together enhances results is essential. When ideas, experiences, and resources are shared, innovative solutions and more effective ways to achieve goals emerge. Sincere partnerships create an environment of mutual support, where everyone benefits and evolves together. This constant cooperation opens doors to opportunities that would hardly be achieved in isolation.

The constant pursuit of personal and professional growth is another fundamental attitude. Investing in the development of new skills and continuous improvement allows you to identify new possibilities and adapt easily to changes. This flexibility in the face of challenges is a differential. Instead of resisting the unexpected, those who cultivate the abundance mindset see changes as valuable chances for evolution, adjusting the path whenever necessary.

Maintaining a long-term vision is also essential. Being clear about the bigger goals guides daily decisions, making them more conscious and strategic. This avoids distractions with immediate results and keeps the focus on what really matters. This future perspective provides serenity and patience, allowing achievements to happen naturally and sustainably.

To nurture this abundance mindset, it is necessary to incorporate daily practices that reinforce this vision. Taking time to reflect on your own achievements, whether big or small, creates a deeper connection with the present. Writing in a journal or verbalizing gratitude helps to consolidate this positive perception. In addition, generosity can be cultivated through simple gestures, such as offering support to those in need or dedicating time to social causes. Each act of kindness contributes to strengthening the cycle of prosperity.

Positive affirmations are another powerful tool. Repeating phrases like "I am worthy of unlimited prosperity" or "Abundance flows naturally to me" reinforces beliefs that support this way of thinking. These words have the power to reprogram mental patterns and strengthen trust in the constant flow of opportunities.

Visualizing the desired success in vivid detail also has a great impact. Imagining yourself achieving goals, feeling the positive emotions associated with these achievements, aligns the subconscious with the actions necessary to make those dreams a reality. This practice creates a mental state conducive to attracting desired circumstances.

Surrounding yourself with positive people is equally important. By living with individuals who share an optimistic vision and celebrate the success of others, it becomes easier to maintain healthy habits and an expansive mindset. At the same time, it is essential to limit exposure to sources of negativity. Filtering content and environments that drain energy helps to preserve emotional and mental balance.

Finally, sincerely celebrating the achievements of others transforms the way success is viewed. By admiring the progress of others, one learns that there is room for everyone to prosper. This sincere recognition reinforces the idea that success is abundant and accessible to all.

These practices, when integrated into everyday life, create a solid foundation for living with more lightness and fullness. The abundance mindset allows you to see life as a fertile field of opportunities, where growth is continuous and the possibilities are endless. Thus, each step taken becomes part of a journey rich in meaning, marked by prosperity, genuine connections, and personal fulfillment.

Trust the flow of life: Cultivate an unshakeable confidence that everything happens at the right time and that the universe is working in your favor. Accept that not everything is under your control, but that every experience contributes to your growth. This faith in the natural process of life brings lightness, reduces anxiety, and allows abundance to manifest fluidly.

By integrating the abundance mindset into everyday life, one realizes that true wealth goes beyond the material. The experiences lived, the relationships built, and the lessons learned form an immeasurable heritage. This understanding allows each challenge to be faced with resilience and creativity, as trust in the constant flow of opportunities brings serenity even in the face of adversity. Thus, the pursuit of growth ceases to be a desperate race and becomes a pleasurable journey of self-discovery and fulfillment.

The abundance mindset also promotes a significant change in the way one deals with time. By realizing that there is room for everything that is essential, it becomes easier to balance commitments and moments of rest. This balance directly reflects on the quality of life, allowing goals to be achieved in a lighter and more sustainable way. The appreciation of the present, without haste for the future or attachment to the past, strengthens the ability to live each moment fully.

Chapter 10
Positive Language

Language directly influences how you perceive and interact with the world, being a fundamental tool for building a more prosperous and harmonious reality. The words you choose daily have the power to shape thoughts, feelings, and behaviors, impacting both the way you relate to yourself and to the people around you. By adopting positive communication, you strengthen your mind with constructive thoughts, promoting more assertive and productive attitudes. This change in vocabulary not only modifies the perception of challenges, but also boosts self-confidence and the ability to find creative solutions. The conscious use of uplifting words creates a solid foundation for transforming obstacles into opportunities and maximizing positive outcomes in various areas of life.

In addition to strengthening the mindset, positive language adjusts your energy frequency, bringing you closer to feelings such as gratitude, enthusiasm, and optimism. This vibrational elevation facilitates the attraction of favorable situations, people aligned with your goals, and opportunities that contribute to personal and professional growth. By expressing words that reflect confidence and hope, you connect with a continuous flow of prosperity and well-being. This energetic alignment is reflected not only in individual achievements, but also in building healthier relationships, based on respect, empathy, and collaboration. Positive communication, therefore, becomes a powerful instrument to create harmonious environments and strengthen interpersonal bonds, promoting mutual development and opening doors to new possibilities.

By incorporating motivating and encouraging words into your internal and external dialogues, you stimulate a broader perception of yourself and the world. This habit transforms the way you interpret challenges, helping you identify solutions and stay focused on desired outcomes. Positive language acts as a catalyst for personal development, reinforcing self-esteem, fueling determination, and increasing clarity of purpose. With this strengthened foundation, it becomes easier to face adversity, set clear goals, and move confidently towards fulfilling dreams. This continuous process of self-transformation allows you to build a more prosperous, fulfilling reality that is aligned with your values and goals.

Imagine yourself as a painter using vibrant and cheerful colors to create a work of art. The colors they choose convey emotions, create atmospheres, and influence the viewer's perception. In the same way, the words you use paint the picture of your reality, coloring your experiences and attracting into your life what you express.

Imagine yourself in front of a vast garden, where every word you utter is like a seed sown in the ground. Kind and encouraging words bloom into beautiful trees and vibrant flowers, while negative words can generate thorns or barren spaces. Just as a gardener carefully chooses the seeds he plants, the way you use language has the power to nurture or limit the growth of your own life. Each positive expression cultivates a fertile environment for the flourishing of opportunities, healthy relationships, and emotional well-being.

Positive language, therefore, is not just a form of communication, but a powerful instrument for transforming realities. By replacing words of doubt and limitation with affirmations of confidence and optimism, you begin to reprogram your subconscious mind. This silent but profound process replaces limiting beliefs with constructive thoughts, creating a solid foundation for more proactive attitudes. This inner change boosts self-confidence and strengthens the ability to act with determination, becoming a pillar for the realization of dreams.

More than an internal impact, positive language also directly influences the energy you emit. Words of gratitude, joy, and hope raise your vibrational frequency, aligning you with situations, people, and opportunities that vibrate in the same tune. This energy flow creates a network of connections that facilitates the path to prosperity. By expressing optimism, you not only attract favorable circumstances, but also inspire those around you to adopt a more constructive stance.

The reflections of this practice are visible in interpersonal relationships. Communication based on respect and kindness strengthens bonds and promotes empathy. Words of encouragement and recognition create environments of trust and collaboration, where ideas flow freely and bonds deepen. In professional environments, this positive climate favors teamwork and boosts productivity. At home, it generates harmony and mutual understanding. Thus, the power of words extends beyond the individual, reaching everyone with whom they connect.

This positive impact is also manifested in the way you face challenges. By cultivating optimistic language, difficulties are no longer seen as insurmountable barriers and are recognized as surmountable challenges. Replacing terms like "problem" with "challenge" or "failure" with "learning" restructures the way you view adverse situations. This simple change in perspective opens space for creative solutions and a resilient stance in the face of difficulties.

Building positive language requires attention and constant practice. Carefully observing internal dialogues is the first step. Often, self-criticism and limiting thoughts arise automatically, influencing actions and decisions. By identifying these patterns, it is possible to interrupt them and replace them with more encouraging expressions. Saying "I can't" can be transformed into "I'm learning," and "this is difficult" into "this is challenging." This adjustment in internal vocabulary strengthens self-confidence and creates a mental space more conducive to growth.

Positive affirmations play a fundamental role in this process. Phrases like "I am capable," "I deserve prosperity," or "every day I am closer to my goals" function as anchors for an abundance mindset. Repeating them with intention reinforces the belief that it is possible to overcome obstacles and achieve goals. Over time, these affirmations become naturally integrated into everyday thinking, influencing decisions and behaviors.

Another powerful practice is choosing words that inspire. Incorporating terms like "growth," "overcoming," and "achievement" into your daily vocabulary stimulates positive emotions and strengthens motivation. This careful selection of words not only elevates your emotional state, but also creates an internal environment favorable to achieving goals. At the same time, eliminating negative and limiting words helps to maintain this positive flow. Replacing "never" with "not yet" and "impossible" with "challenging" broadens horizons and encourages the search for solutions.

Expressing gratitude is another essential element in building positive language. Giving thanks for achievements, experiences, and even challenges strengthens the perception of abundance. This habit creates a virtuous cycle: the more you recognize and value what you have, the more reasons you find to be grateful. This genuine feeling of gratitude attracts new opportunities and strengthens the connection with the present.

In addition to taking care of the words directed at yourself, it is also important to spread positivity around you. Sincerely praising, offering words of support, and encouraging people creates a welcoming and stimulating environment. Small gestures, such as recognizing someone's effort or celebrating their achievements, have the power to strengthen bonds and inspire positive change. This behavior generates a multiplier effect, encouraging others to also adopt more constructive communication.

Clarity and assertiveness in communication are also fundamental. Expressing ideas and feelings in an objective, respectful, and safe way avoids misunderstandings and strengthens relationships. This balance between firmness and empathy allows you to establish healthy boundaries and build authentic connections. Assertive communication opens space for productive dialogues and relationships based on mutual trust.

Avoiding complaints and gossip is equally important. Participating in constructive and enriching conversations preserves personal energy and contributes to a lighter and more positive environment. Consciously choosing interactions that bring learning and inspiration strengthens the positive mindset and favors growth.

Finally, feeding the mind with uplifting content completes this process. Reading motivational books, watching inspiring movies, and seeking knowledge that expands your worldview are ways to nurture your mind with ideas that stimulate growth. This constant habit broadens perspectives, brings new ideas, and reinforces the connection with elevated emotions.

By integrating positive language into your routine, you not only transform the way you think and act, but also create a lasting positive impact on the environment around you. Each conscious word is a seed that blossoms into attitudes, decisions, and results. This silent power shapes behaviors, inspires change, and strengthens relationships. Thus, you become not only the protagonist of your own story, but also an agent of transformation in the world.

Over time, this practice becomes consolidated as a natural habit, influencing all areas of life. Positive communication becomes a reflection of a strengthened mindset, capable of facing challenges with resilience and seeking opportunities with enthusiasm. Awareness of the power of words allows you to build a path of authentic achievements, deep relationships, and a life aligned with your values.

Thus, by choosing your words with intention and purpose, you take control of your personal narrative. Each sentence spoken with confidence and positivity contributes to the construction of a lighter, fuller, and more abundant reality. True transformation begins when you understand that the way you communicate has the power to create, strengthen, and expand everything you want to experience.

By integrating positive language into your routine, you not only transform your mindset, but also influence the environment around you in a significant way. Each word chosen with intention carries with it the power to generate impact, shaping behaviors and inspiring those with whom you interact. This subtle but profound power enhances your ability to lead by example, creating a network of positive influence that reverberates in all spheres of your life. Thus, communication becomes a channel of genuine connection, capable of stimulating collective growth and strengthening bonds based on respect and empathy.

Over time, the constant practice of positive language is consolidated as an essential pillar for emotional balance and well-being. This habit allows you to reframe past experiences and face the present with more lightness and clarity, cultivating resilience in the face of challenges. By replacing self-limiting thoughts with encouraging affirmations, you activate your creative potential and find motivation to move forward with purpose. This silent but consistent transformation is reflected in your daily actions, making the journey more rewarding and meaningful.

By understanding that each word has the power to create or limit, you take control of your personal narrative. From this awareness, positive communication ceases to be just a choice and becomes a natural expression of your essence. Thus, you build a trajectory marked by authentic achievements, enriching relationships, and a life aligned with your deepest values. This path of continuous evolution reveals that true abundance is born from the way we choose to communicate with the world and, above all, with ourselves.

Chapter 11
Energy Cleansing

Energy cleansing is an essential practice to maintain the balance of body, mind, and spirit, promoting well-being and harmony in all aspects of life. Just as it is essential to take care of physical hygiene and the environment in which we live, it is equally necessary to ensure the purity of our energy. By removing negative charges and blockages accumulated over time, a continuous flow of vital energy is created that favors health, prosperity, and happiness. This process allows energy to circulate freely, raising personal vibration and opening space for new opportunities and positive experiences.

The accumulation of dense and stagnant energies can directly impact emotional, mental, and physical balance, influencing how we face daily challenges and interact with the world around us. Regular energy purification practices help restore well-being, revitalize disposition, and strengthen the connection with one's life purpose. Methods such as energy baths, meditation, the use of crystals, and smudging are effective tools for dissolving blockages, cleansing the vibrational field, and re-establishing the natural flow of vital energy.

Keeping the energy clean and balanced not only strengthens the body and mind but also enhances the ability to attract abundance, health, and harmonious relationships. From a consistent routine of energy care, it is possible to perceive significant transformations in the quality of life, emotions, and thoughts. By integrating these practices into everyday life, we create a lighter and more positive internal and external environment, favoring personal and spiritual growth.

Imagine a crystalline river, whose waters flow freely, reflecting sunlight on its surface. This river, however, can, over time, accumulate dry leaves, broken branches, and other debris that interrupt its natural flow. The water, once clear and full of life, becomes cloudy and heavy. Just like this river, our energy can also be affected by blockages and impurities that accumulate over time. Energy cleansing emerges as a way to remove these invisible obstacles, allowing vital energy to flow again with strength, clarity, and vitality.

Our daily interactions with environments, people, and situations constantly expose us to different types of energy. We absorb not only positive vibrations but also those that are denser and more charged. Arguments, disorganized environments, negative thoughts, and repressed emotions are common sources of energy accumulation. When this negative charge is not properly released, it can manifest as extreme tiredness, irritability, relationship difficulties, and even blockages that impede the natural flow of abundance in our lives.

Energy cleansing works deeply in these aspects, promoting a true renewal on several levels. On the physical plane, practices such as energy baths and massages with essential oils dissipate accumulated tensions in the body, relieving unexplained pain and restoring disposition. In the emotional field, meditation techniques, the use of crystals, and the practice of yoga are effective in releasing repressed emotions, such as sadness, anger, and fear, bringing lightness and emotional clarity. On the mental level, methods such as positive affirmations and creative visualizations help dissolve negative thoughts and repetitive patterns, opening space for new ideas and more assertive actions. In the spiritual aspect, rituals of prayer, connection with nature, and energy therapies, such as Reiki, strengthen the connection with the purpose of life and raise the personal vibration, favoring the manifestation of prosperity and well-being.

The signs that an energy cleansing is needed are varied and often subtle. Excessive tiredness, even after rest, can be a clear indication that there is an energy overload preventing the natural flow of vitality. Physical pain without apparent cause, insomnia, anxiety, and irritability are other warning signs. In addition, persistent difficulties in areas such as finances, relationships, and health can also be a reflection of energy blockages that need to be dissolved. Recognizing these signs is critical to beginning the purification process and reconnecting with the natural flow of life.

Among the most effective methods of energy cleansing are baths with herbs and coarse salt, which act as powerful purifiers. Contact with natural elements, such as seawater or earth, also has a restorative effect, helping to discharge dense energies. Smudging with herbs like sage, rue, and rosemary cleanses not only the personal energy field but also the environment, creating a lighter and more welcoming atmosphere. The use of crystals, such as black tourmaline for protection and amethyst for transmuting negative energies, is another valuable practice. These crystals absorb and balance the vibrations around us, promoting harmony and well-being.

Meditation is a powerful tool for calming the mind and releasing emotional tension. Visualization techniques, such as imagining a golden or violet light enveloping the body and dissolving blockages, are effective in restoring energy balance. Spiritual practices, such as sincere prayer, help create a field of protection and attract inner peace. Reiki, a therapy that channels universal energy through the hands, acts directly on unblocking energy points, promoting deep relaxation and integral balance.

Integrating these energy cleansing methods into your routine brings benefits that go beyond immediate relief. With constant practice, it is possible to perceive a significant improvement in the quality of life, relationships, and mental clarity. Energy flows more lightly, favoring more conscious decision-making and the creation of an internal environment conducive to personal and spiritual growth. This state of balance facilitates the achievement of goals and the realization of dreams, as it removes invisible barriers that previously blocked the way.

In addition to cleansing practices, maintaining high energy requires daily care. Cultivating positive thoughts is essential to preserve a clean and protected energy field. Avoiding complaints, gossip, and excessive criticism prevents the creation of unnecessary blockages. Practicing gratitude daily expands the perception of abundance, reinforcing a high vibration. Surrounding yourself with positive and inspiring people also contributes to maintaining light and fluid energy.

Caring for the physical body, through a balanced diet and regular physical activity, is also essential. Fresh, natural foods, rich in nutrients, strengthen vital energy. Physical exercise helps release accumulated tension and stimulates energy flow. Keeping the environment clean, organized, and well-ventilated is another important practice. Disorganized spaces accumulate stagnant energy, while light and harmonious environments favor the circulation of good energies.

Aromatherapy is an excellent ally in this process. Essential oils of lavender, rosemary, eucalyptus, and sweet orange have properties that cleanse and energize the environment and personal aura. Diffusers, sprays, or a few drops on the pillow can transform the mood of the space, promoting relaxation and focus.

Incorporating practices such as listening to mantras or high-frequency music also helps in raising vibration. Sacred sounds act directly on the harmonization of the chakras, balancing body, mind, and spirit. Walking in nature, feeling the wind, touching the earth, or simply contemplating natural beauty are simple and effective ways to renew energy.

When energy is clean and flowing freely, interpersonal relationships are also transformed. Inner lightness is reflected in the way we communicate, making dialogues clearer and more respectful. Emotional bonds are strengthened, conflicts are resolved more easily, and new connections, more aligned with our values, arise naturally. This balance facilitates the creation of authentic and harmonious relationships, based on empathy and mutual understanding.

Finally, energy cleansing is an invitation to live with more lightness, clarity, and purpose. Each practice performed with intention strengthens the connection with one's own essence and opens space for enriching experiences. With energy flowing in a balanced way, it becomes easier to deal with challenges, recognize opportunities, and follow a path of personal and spiritual fulfillment. Just as a river that flows freely again after being unblocked, life becomes more abundant and full when we take care of our energy with attention and care.

By adopting energy cleansing practices consistently, we create a cycle of continuous renewal that positively impacts all aspects of life. This care not only eliminates blockages and dense energies but also strengthens the connection with the present, allowing a clearer perception of the opportunities around us. Thus, energy flows with lightness, favoring more conscious choices and actions aligned with our purposes. This harmonious flow drives us to act with confidence, creating a more fluid path to achieve goals and realize dreams.

The transformation provided by energy cleansing is also reflected in the way we relate to the world. Interpersonal connections become more authentic and balanced, as renewed energy attracts people and situations that vibrate in tune with our well-being. This balance facilitates conflict resolution, strengthens emotional bonds, and expands the ability to express feelings in a healthy way. With a peaceful mind and a light heart, we cultivate more harmonious relationships, based on understanding, respect, and mutual support.

Finally, incorporating energy cleansing as part of daily self-care is an invitation to live more fully and consciously. Each practice, whether simple or elaborate, contributes to strengthening our essence, protecting us from negative influences and opening space for growth and prosperity. With clean energy flowing freely, we become more resilient in the face of challenges and more receptive to the blessings that life has to offer, allowing the personal journey to be conducted with balance, clarity, and purpose.

Chapter 12
Crystals and Abundance

Crystals are natural sources of energy, formed over millions of years in the depths of the Earth, carrying in their composition unique vibrational properties that directly influence the human energy field. These precious stones have the ability to channel and amplify positive frequencies, being effective instruments to attract prosperity, emotional balance, and physical well-being. When used with intention and purpose, crystals become powerful tools for the manifestation of abundance in various areas of life, acting as bridges between the material world and the subtle energies that surround us. Their crystalline structure resonates with the vibrations of the universe, creating a synergy that favors the flow of positive energies, allowing desires and goals to materialize in a more fluid and harmonious way.

By integrating crystals into everyday life, it is possible to access their specific properties to boost personal and professional goals. Each type of crystal vibrates at a distinct frequency, aligning with different intentions and needs. For example, stones like Citrine are known to stimulate financial prosperity and success, while Rose Quartz promotes love and harmony in relationships. The interaction with these minerals favors the elevation of personal energy frequency, creating a conducive field for attracting opportunities and overcoming challenges. Thus, by consciously selecting and using a crystal aligned with a specific purpose, the person strengthens their connection with the energies of abundance, enhancing the achievement of their goals.

The practice of using crystals involves more than simply having them around; it requires care, clear intention, and emotional connection. From the intuitive choice of stone to its cleansing, energizing, and programming with specific desires, each step of this process contributes to enhancing the energy of the crystal. Incorporating them into the daily routine, whether as accessories, decorative objects, or meditation tools, creates a continuous flow of positive vibrations. This conscious involvement allows not only to attract prosperity but also to maintain energy balance, strengthening self-confidence, mental clarity, and motivation. In this way, crystals become essential allies in building a full, abundant life aligned with the best opportunities the universe has to offer.

Imagine holding a crystal in your hands, feeling its cool, smooth texture as a slight vibration runs through your fingers. This simple gesture carries profound power, for crystals are more than just beautiful stones; they are true manifestations of Earth's energy, accumulating vibrations over millions of years. Just as an antenna tunes into invisible frequencies, a crystal amplifies and channels subtle energies, connecting you to universal forces that directly influence the flow of prosperity and balance in your life. Using crystals with conscious intention is like opening a direct channel to the manifestation of abundance in all areas of existence.

This connection between crystals and abundance is strengthened by the synergy with the Law of Attraction, which teaches us that like attracts like. Each crystal vibrates at a specific frequency, and by choosing a stone aligned with your purpose, you tune your energy with what you want to attract. If the intention is financial prosperity, Citrine, with its warm and expansive vibration, acts as a powerful magnet for wealth. To strengthen loving relationships, Rose Quartz vibrates at the frequency of love and harmony, promoting deep and authentic connections. This energetic interaction does not occur randomly, but as a result of an intentional alignment between the person's purpose and the vibration of the chosen crystal.

The conscious use of crystals requires more than simply keeping them around. It is necessary to establish a true connection with them, involving important steps such as intuitive choice, energy cleansing, energizing, and programming with clear intentions. This process begins from the moment of selection. When coming into contact with various crystals, it is important to allow intuition to guide the choice. Often, a specific stone draws attention, causes a feeling of warmth, or simply "stands out" from the others. This is a sign that the vibration of the crystal is in tune with your energy and your needs at that moment.

After selection, energy cleansing is essential to purify the crystal of any previous influences. Crystals absorb and accumulate energies from the environment and people, so they need to be cleaned before being programmed with new intentions. Simple methods such as smudging with herbs, immersion in water with coarse salt (respecting the characteristics of each stone), or exposure to sunlight or moonlight are effective in restoring their vibrational purity. After this purification, energizing the crystal enhances its performance. Sunlight revitalizes solar crystals, such as Citrine and Pyrite, while moonlight intensifies the energy of more subtle and introspective stones, such as Amethyst and Rose Quartz.

The next step is to program the crystal with the desired intention. Holding the stone firmly, close your eyes and clearly visualize what you want to manifest. Imagine this intention being absorbed by the crystal, which then radiates this energy around you. This act of programming transforms the crystal into an active ally in the manifestation of your goals, creating a continuous flow of energy focused on what you seek to achieve.

There are several specific crystals to attract abundance and prosperity, each with unique properties that act on different aspects of life. Citrine, known as the "stone of prosperity", carries the energy of the sun, radiating enthusiasm, confidence, and creativity. Its vibration stimulates motivation and mental clarity, facilitating the overcoming of challenges and the achievement of financial goals. Pyrite, with its golden glow, symbolizes wealth and power. In addition to attracting financial opportunities, this stone protects against negative energies and stimulates logical reasoning, making it an excellent ally for entrepreneurs and professionals seeking growth.

Tiger's Eye, in turn, balances courage and protection. This stone helps to make wise decisions and avoid unnecessary risks, providing security and determination in times of challenge. Green Aventurine, known as the "stone of luck", opens paths to new opportunities and promotes prosperity in a balanced way. Its gentle energy calms emotions and strengthens confidence, favoring more conscious decisions. Jade, an ancient symbol of luck and abundance, emanates a vibration of stability and lasting growth. Associated with wisdom and prosperity, this stone encourages wise decisions and protects against negative influences.

Incorporating crystals into everyday life is simple and powerful. Carrying a stone in your pocket or wearing it as an accessory keeps its energy in constant contact with your body. Meditating with the crystal in your hands or placing it on the corresponding chakra enhances the connection with the intention. Decorating environments with strategic crystals also harmonizes the energy of the space. For example, placing a Pyrite in the workplace attracts business prosperity, while a Citrine in the wealth corner (according to Feng Shui) enhances financial gains.

Crystal maintenance is also essential to ensure their continued effectiveness. Just as we cleanse our body and mind, crystals need to be cleansed regularly to release accumulated energies. Incorporating practices of gratitude and respect for the crystal further strengthens this connection. Thanking the stone for its energetic action reinforces the flow of prosperity, creating a relationship of exchange and respect.

Also, it is important to remember that abundance is not just about financial gain. True prosperity involves emotional balance, physical well-being, harmony in relationships, and spiritual growth. Crystals act in an integrated way, providing balance in all these areas. Amethyst, for example, elevates spirituality and calms the mind, while Green Quartz promotes health and emotional healing. This complete balance allows abundance to manifest in a fluid and sustainable way.

Continuous practice with crystals also inspires daily habits of presence and gratitude, which are fundamental to maintaining a high vibration. Recognizing and valuing small achievements strengthens the path to greater achievements. The energy of crystals, coupled with an open and intentional mindset, creates an internal and external environment conducive to growth. This harmony between intention, action, and energy vibration enhances the manifestation of goals and the construction of a full life.

By integrating crystals into your journey, not just as decorative objects, but as energy allies, you open space for prosperity to flow naturally. This balance between the material and spiritual world allows you to access new possibilities, transform challenges into learning, and live with more confidence and purpose. Each crystal chosen, programmed, and cared for with intention becomes a silent but powerful partner in building a life rich in abundance, harmony, and fulfillment.

By deepening this connection with crystals, it is important to remember that true abundance is not limited to material possessions, but also encompasses emotional, spiritual, and mental fulfillment. The energy emanating from crystals favors not only the manifestation of tangible riches but also the expansion of consciousness and the strengthening of self-knowledge. By cultivating an open and receptive mindset, aligned with the energies of crystals, a continuous flow of opportunities is created, where prosperity manifests naturally and in a balanced way in all areas of life.

Furthermore, the conscious use of crystals inspires daily practices of gratitude and presence, essential elements to maintain a high vibration and attract positive experiences. This process encourages the individual to recognize and value small daily achievements, creating a solid foundation for greater achievements. The harmony between intention, action, and the energy of crystals strengthens the path to a more abundant life, where each choice reflects a commitment to personal growth and the creation of a prosperous and balanced environment.

Thus, by integrating crystals into your journey, not just as tools, but as true energy allies, you open space for abundance to flow with lightness and purpose. This balance between the material and spiritual world allows you to access new possibilities, transform challenges into learning, and build a reality based on trust, harmony, and continuous prosperity.

Chapter 13
Vibrational Aromatherapy

Vibrational aromatherapy enhances physical, emotional, and energetic balance through the conscious use of essential oils, which carry the life force of plants. These natural compounds, extracted from flowers, roots, bark, and leaves, act directly on the harmonization of body and mind, raising the vibrational frequency and facilitating the manifestation of abundance in various areas of life. The interaction between aromas and the brain's limbic system triggers positive responses that promote well-being, unlock limiting patterns, and stimulate energy flow, allowing alignment with states of prosperity, love, and inner peace. Thus, vibrational aromatherapy presents itself as a transformative practice, capable of integrating the wisdom of nature with emotional and spiritual balance.

Essential oils have unique properties that reverberate in different aspects of existence, being able to influence emotions, thoughts, and behaviors. When applied with intention, these oils attune the mind to the energy of prosperity, health, and personal fulfillment. Sweet orange oil, for example, is known for its vibration of joy and expansion, dissolving emotional blocks and awakening creativity, while lavender oil promotes calm and emotional balance, creating an internal environment conducive to personal growth. This direct connection between aroma and energy vibration transforms vibrational aromatherapy into an effective tool to attract abundance, unlock potential, and favor the flow of opportunities.

By integrating vibrational aromatherapy into your daily routine, it is possible to strengthen the connection between body, mind, and energy, enhancing results in various areas of life. The practice goes beyond simply inhaling pleasant aromas; it is a conscious process of aligning thoughts, emotions, and intentions with the vital energy of nature. The application of essential oils, whether by inhalation, massage, baths, or diffusers, creates a high vibrational field, favoring inner harmony and attracting experiences aligned with desires for prosperity and fulfillment. Thus, vibrational aromatherapy is consolidated as a natural and powerful way to transform personal energy, open space for new possibilities, and live more fully and abundantly.

Imagine yourself walking through a vast garden, where the air is impregnated with the scent of flowers swaying gently in the wind. Each deep breath brings with it a feeling of serenity and vitality, as if nature itself were whispering secrets of balance and renewal. This environment not only relaxes but also invigorates, awakening a subtle and powerful energy that runs through the entire body. Just like this walk among fragrant flowers, the use of essential oils in vibrational aromatherapy acts in a similar way, raising the energy vibration, balancing emotions, and opening paths for abundance to manifest in a fluid and natural way.

The connection between essential oils and the frequency of abundance is deep and intuitive. Each essence carries a unique vibration that interacts directly with different aspects of life. By using these oils with clear intention and defined purpose, an energy bridge is created between desire and its fulfillment. It is like tuning into a specific radio station: by adjusting to the correct frequency, the music flows without interference. Thus, when choosing an essential oil aligned with what one seeks to manifest - be it prosperity, health, love, or inner peace - the energy around begins to reorganize itself to support these goals.

Among the many essential oils available, some are especially known for their ability to attract abundance. Sweet orange essential oil, with its citrusy and vibrant aroma, is a true invitation to joy and enthusiasm. Its fragrance has the power to dissolve emotional blocks and stimulate creativity, allowing new ideas and opportunities to flourish with lightness. Inhaling its aroma or applying it to the skin is like a wave of positivity and expansive energy invading the environment, creating space for the natural flow of prosperity.

The warm intensity of cinnamon essential oil, in turn, awakens a fiery life force. Its potent vibration strengthens self-confidence and determination, creating an energy field conducive to financial growth and business success. The striking aroma of cinnamon is like a flame that ignites motivation, driving action and attracting opportunities for material prosperity. This vibrant energy is ideal for times when it is necessary to make bold decisions or seek professional expansion.

With its earthy and deep aroma, patchouli essential oil invites connection with the energy of the Earth. This essence promotes stability and security, fundamental to transforming desires into concrete reality. The feeling of grounding provided by patchouli strengthens the emotional base, allowing projects and dreams to be built with solidity. Its dense and welcoming vibration creates an internal environment of trust and resilience, facilitating the materialization of goals.

Ginger, with its warm, spicy aroma, brings a vibrant energy that inspires courage and initiative. This essential oil acts as an impulse for immediate action, dissolving fears and hesitations that may be blocking the path to prosperity. Its energetic presence encourages you to step out of your comfort zone and face challenges with determination, opening doors to new opportunities in all areas of life.

The herbal freshness of basil essential oil clears the mind and sharpens focus. Its mental influence provides a lucidity that facilitates assertive decision-making, essential for success in business and projects. This state of mental clarity and emotional balance creates ideal conditions for financial prosperity to manifest consistently and sustainably. Basil, with its light and revitalizing energy, helps to overcome mental obstacles, allowing ideas to flow with clarity and objectivity.

Finally, ylang ylang essential oil, with its floral and exotic fragrance, promotes self-love and self-confidence. Its gentle essence opens the heart to harmonious relationships and strengthens the connection with emotional and material abundance. When enveloped in this delicate aroma, one perceives an invitation to surrender and to the flow of love in all its forms. This loving and receptive energy facilitates the receiving of prosperity, allowing love and abundance to flow freely.

Integrating these essential oils into your daily routine can be a profoundly transformative experience. Direct inhalation, for example, provides immediate effects, whether by deeply breathing the aroma directly from the bottle or using a diffuser to spread the fragrance throughout the environment. This simple act of intentionally breathing in an aroma can alter emotional states and raise energy vibration, creating a space conducive to well-being and goal achievement.

Massages with essential oils are another powerful way to incorporate these benefits. By diluting a few drops in a carrier vegetable oil and applying to the skin with gentle movements, not only are muscles relaxed, but the absorption of the therapeutic properties of the essence is also facilitated. This direct contact with the body intensifies the connection between mind, emotion, and vital energy, promoting balance and stimulating the flow of prosperity.

Transforming bathing into a self-care ritual also enhances the effects of vibrational aromatherapy. By adding drops of essential oil diluted in vegetable oil or honey to warm water, the aromatic steam envelops the body, providing deep relaxation and energy renewal. This intimate moment becomes an opportunity for purification, where tensions are dissolved and intentions of abundance are strengthened.

Aromatic compresses offer targeted and effective care. Applying a cloth soaked in water flavored with essential oils to specific areas of the body helps relieve pain, reduce tension, and unblock energy points. This simple method enhances physical and emotional balance, creating a vibrational field aligned with prosperity.

The use of personal diffusers, such as diffuser necklaces and bracelets, allows you to carry the energy of essential oils throughout the day. Applying small drops to these accessories creates a constant connection with the intentions of emotional balance and abundance. Thus, even in the midst of the daily rush, it is possible to stay centered and aligned with your purposes.

To further enhance the effects of vibrational aromatherapy, it is essential to choose high quality essential oils. Choosing pure products, free of additives and from brands committed to sustainable practices, ensures the integrity of the therapeutic properties. Proper dilution in carrier oils ensures safety in topical use, avoiding irritation and promoting effective absorption.

More importantly, it is the conscious and intentional use of oils. Mentalizing specific goals during application amplifies the vibrational frequency, creating a synergy between thoughts, emotions, and the energy of the essences. Combining different oils that complement each other also enhances their effects, creating an even stronger and more directed vibration.

By allowing each aroma to intuitively guide the process of self-knowledge and transformation, vibrational aromatherapy becomes a powerful tool for reconnecting with one's own essence. Incorporating this practice with purpose opens a portal to richer and more authentic experiences, allowing abundance to flow naturally and harmoniously in all aspects of life.

By deepening the practice of vibrational aromatherapy, it is essential to cultivate an intuitive connection with essential oils, allowing each aroma to guide the process of self-knowledge and transformation. This intimate bond with natural fragrances not only enhances their energetic benefits, but also awakens a sensitive listening to the needs of the body and soul. By recognizing which essences resonate most intensely at different times in life, it becomes possible to adjust the practice in a personalized way, respecting the natural flow of emotions and intentions.

In addition, integrating simple rituals into everyday life, such as moments of meditation with diffusers or the creation of sacred environments with specific aromas, amplifies the vibrational power of essential oils. These small gestures of self-care cultivate an inner space of clarity and receptivity, facilitating the manifestation of desires and goals. The combination of conscious intention with the use of essential oils strengthens the attunement with universal abundance, promoting a journey of continuous growth and full balance.

Thus, vibrational aromatherapy is revealed as more than a wellness practice: it is a path of reconnection with the essence of life, where each aroma carries a message from nature to nourish body, mind, and spirit. By incorporating this ancestral wisdom with presence and purpose, a portal is opened to richer and more authentic experiences, allowing abundance to flow naturally and harmoniously in all aspects of existence.

Chapter 14
Feng Shui for Prosperity

Feng Shui is a practice deeply rooted in ancient Chinese wisdom, recognized for its ability to transform environments into spaces of balance and harmony. By applying its principles, it is possible to adjust the energy of environments in order to favor the flow of Chi, the vital energy responsible for nourishing all areas of life. This art seeks to promote harmonious integration between human beings and the space around them, positively influencing aspects such as prosperity, health, love, and well-being. Through subtle adjustments in the arrangement of furniture, choice of colors, inclusion of natural elements, and removal of energy blocks, Feng Shui offers practical and effective tools to attract abundance and opportunities. Each detail in the environment is treated as a fundamental piece to create a continuous and positive energy flow, capable of reflecting and amplifying intentions for growth and success.

The harmony of physical space is directly connected to emotional and financial balance. When energy circulates freely and without obstacles, the home or work environment becomes a reflection of stability and prosperity. Elements such as healthy plants, adequate lighting, and symbolic objects of wealth are used strategically to strengthen this connection. The organized arrangement of furniture, the conscious choice of colors, and the integration of natural elements are aspects that transform the environment into a channel of attraction for good opportunities. Thus, Feng Shui not only beautifies spaces, but also energetically aligns them with clear goals of prosperity and personal fulfillment.

By understanding the interaction between natural elements and physical space, it becomes possible to create environments that stimulate motivation, creativity, and emotional balance. Each adjustment made with intention, whether at the entrance of the house, in the choice of decorative objects, or in the arrangement of furniture, directly influences the quality of the energy that circulates. Feng Shui offers a practical and accessible path for those seeking to align their material and emotional life with the natural flow of abundance. Thus, by transforming the environment into a welcoming and vibrant space, it is possible to open doors to new possibilities and achieve a state of complete well-being, where prosperity and balance go hand in hand.

Imagine your house as a living organism, pulsating and full of energy, where each room plays an essential role in the overall harmony. The vital energy, known as "Chi" in Feng Shui, flows freely through the spaces, nourishing each environment and directly influencing the well-being and prosperity of the residents. Just as blood circulates through the body, carrying nutrients and vitality, Chi flows through the rooms, distributing balance and abundance. However, this flow can be interrupted by energy blocks caused by clutter, broken objects, or improper furniture arrangement. Feng Shui teaches you to identify these blocks and transform them, creating a positive and continuous energy flow that favors growth, prosperity, and well-being in all areas of life.

In Feng Shui, the energy of prosperity is closely linked to the wood element, a symbol of growth, renewal, and expansion. To activate this energy at home, it is essential to create an environment that allows Chi to flow without obstacles. Organization and cleanliness are the first steps in this process. Disorganized spaces accumulate stagnant energy, hindering the flow of opportunities. By eliminating broken objects, unused items, and unnecessary excesses, you make room for energy to circulate freely. Airy and organized environments function as channels through which the energy of prosperity can enter and expand. Each object in the house carries a vibration that influences emotional state and financial life, so taking care of every detail is essential to create a prosperous environment.

Colors also play a fundamental role in harmonizing spaces and attracting prosperity. Shades of green represent growth and renewal, while blue conveys serenity and emotional balance. Both are related to the wood element and are powerful activators of abundance energy. Adding touches of black or dark blue complements this flow, as these tones represent the water element, which nourishes wood and stimulates prosperity. Walls painted in soft green, blue pillows, or decorative objects in these shades help to create a harmonious environment, capable of enhancing energy flow. The combination of these colors should be done with balance, always respecting the overall harmony of the space.

Live plants are natural symbols of vitality and growth and play an essential role in activating prosperity energy. Species such as lucky bamboo, jade plant, and peace lily are especially effective in attracting abundance. Placing them in the far left corner from the front door - known as the wealth sector - enhances their effect. Plants should be healthy, well-cared for, and receive adequate natural light. It is important to avoid species with pointed or thorny leaves, as these can generate aggressive energy, compromising the positive flow. Constant care of plants symbolizes the attention dedicated to financial and personal growth.

Mirrors are powerful tools in Feng Shui, capable of expanding and redirecting energy flow. When strategically positioned, they reflect natural light and duplicate images of prosperity, symbolizing the expansion of abundance. However, they should be used with caution. Avoid placing them in front of the front door, as they can reflect positive energy back out. Prefer to position them so as to reflect pleasant landscapes or objects that symbolize wealth, such as healthy plants or works of art that evoke prosperity. This simple adjustment enhances the feeling of expansion and harmony in the environment.

The introduction of symbolic objects of prosperity is another effective strategy. Functioning water fountains represent the constant flow of money and opportunities. Chinese coins tied with red ribbons and statues of the Buddha of prosperity are traditional symbols that evoke luck and abundance. Paintings that portray scenarios of abundance, such as green landscapes and fertile fields, visually reinforce the intention to attract wealth. These items should be placed in visible locations and harmoniously integrated into the decoration, without exaggeration that could overload the environment. The choice of each object must reflect a clear intention to attract prosperity and well-being.

The front door of the house, in Feng Shui, is considered the "mouth of Chi", through which vital energy enters the environment. Therefore, it is essential that it be inviting and always in good condition. It should be kept clean, with the paint preserved and functional doorknobs. Adequate lighting and decorative elements such as wind chimes or plant pots can make the entrance more welcoming. Obstacles such as furniture or vases that block the way should be avoided, as they prevent the energy of prosperity from flowing freely into the house. A new and well-maintained doormat also symbolizes welcome and enhances energy flow.

The prosperity sector, located in the far left corner from the main entrance, deserves special attention. Decorating this space with golden objects, stones such as pyrite or citrine, and soft lighting helps to activate the energy of abundance. Vibrant plants, pictures with images of success, and elements that represent wealth complete the ideal composition of this corner. The integration of bright colors, natural materials, and symbols of abundance creates a powerful environment to attract financial growth and new opportunities.

In the kitchen, considered the heart of the home and an important center of prosperity, cleanliness and organization are fundamental. The stove should always be clean and with all burners working, representing multiple sources of income. A fruit bowl full of fresh fruit symbolizes abundance, while the use of colors such as red, gold, or green in decorations reinforces the energy of abundance. Damaged appliances should be repaired or replaced, as they represent financial blockages. Attention to detail in the kitchen directly reflects the fluidity of prosperity in the home.

The dining room, as a space for socializing and sharing, also influences family prosperity. Round or oval tables are preferable, as they facilitate the flow of energy and promote harmony. A centerpiece with fruit or fresh flowers symbolizes abundance and vitality. Strategically placed mirrors can duplicate the image of the set table, symbolically amplifying abundance. The lighting should be soft and welcoming, creating a pleasant environment for moments of celebration and togetherness.

For those seeking professional prosperity, the office should be an organized and inspiring environment. The desk should be in the command position, allowing a view of the door without being directly aligned with it, conveying security and control.

A comfortable chair, few items on the desk, and the use of small plants bring vitality. Decorative objects such as globes, images of success, or golden details reinforce the energy of growth and achievement.

Finally, taking care of your wallet and personal finances is also part of Feng Shui practice. Keeping your wallet organized, with bills aligned and without unnecessary papers, symbolizes respect for money. Choosing colors such as green, gold, or red enhances the attraction of prosperity. Keeping symbols of wealth inside it, such as Chinese coins or folded bills, strengthens the flow of abundance.

With these cares and adjustments, Feng Shui becomes a powerful tool to harmonize environments and pave the way for success. Each detail adjusted with intention strengthens the connection with prosperity, allowing energy to flow freely and bring balance, well-being, and continuous growth.

Maintaining the energy of prosperity active requires constancy and attention to the details of everyday life. Small daily habits, such as opening the windows in the morning to renew the air, lighting soft incense, or rearranging objects as needed, reinforce the positive flow of Chi. In addition, the practice of genuine gratitude for the goods and achievements already achieved creates a vibrational field conducive to new opportunities. This balance between practical actions and mental intention strengthens the connection with abundance, making the environment not only beautiful, but also a true magnet for prosperity.

It is important to remember that each adjustment made to the environment must reflect your personality and your goals. Feng Shui is not just a rigid formula, but a practice that should be adapted to your reality, respecting your personal taste and life context. Thus, each choice, from the arrangement of furniture to the selection of symbols of wealth, must carry meaning and intention. By customizing spaces with awareness, you create an authentic environment where energy circulates freely and aligns with your desires for growth and fulfillment.

With these principles integrated into your daily life, prosperity ceases to be just a distant concept and manifests itself concretely in your life. Feng Shui, when applied with sensitivity and purpose, transforms the home into a clear reflection of your dreams and goals, expanding the potential for success in all areas. In this way, the harmony between environment, mind, and spirit becomes the solid foundation for a path of continuous abundance and lasting well-being.

Chapter 15
Music and Frequencies

Music exerts a profound and direct influence on the mind, body, and spirit, acting as a natural bridge between human emotions and the vibrations of the universe. Each sound, rhythm, and melody carries a specific frequency capable of interacting with our emotional and energetic states, promoting balance, well-being, and personal transformation. When used intentionally, music becomes a powerful tool to raise internal vibration, restore harmony to energy centers, and strengthen the connection to the abundance present in all areas of life. This sonic interaction is not limited to entertainment but expands as an effective means of aligning thoughts and feelings with the positive energies that favor prosperity and personal fulfillment.

Musical sounds, when chosen with purpose, have the power to create atmospheres conducive to relaxation, concentration, and emotional growth. The combination of notes, chords, and rhythms can stimulate states of deep calm or motivate concrete actions, depending on the frequency at which they vibrate. Thus, exploring different musical genres and natural sounds allows you to adjust the internal vibration according to the needs of the moment, whether to calm the agitated mind, inspire creativity, or attract positive experiences. The conscious connection with these sounds enhances vital energy, favoring mental clarity, emotional health, and spiritual harmony.

By integrating music into everyday life in an attentive and directed way, a vibrational environment favorable to the manifestation of desires and goals is created. This process involves listening to compositions that resonate with feelings of gratitude, joy, and peace, amplifying the flow of positive energies. Songs with inspiring lyrics, soft melodies, or engaging rhythms reinforce constructive beliefs and unlock limiting patterns, allowing the energy of abundance to flow naturally. Thus, music is revealed not only as art but as an essential resource to nourish the soul, expand consciousness, and attract prosperity in all aspects of life.

Imagine a symphony orchestra playing in perfect harmony. Each instrument, with its unique melody and rhythm, contributes to the creation of a grand symphony that moves and inspires those who listen to it. Just as an orchestra balances itself through the combination of sounds, music can be used as a powerful tool to harmonize the body's energy centers, calm the mind, and attract prosperity and well-being. Sound vibrations travel through our being, aligning emotions, thoughts, and energies, creating a continuous flow of balance and expansion. When we consciously connect with these musical frequencies, we open the way to transform our emotions and tune in to states of abundance and fulfillment.

Music, when associated with the Law of Attraction, becomes even more potent. According to this principle, "like attracts like", which means that we vibrate at the frequency of the experiences and situations that we attract into our lives. Each song has its own vibration, and by choosing melodies that resonate with the energy of prosperity, we begin to tune in to opportunities and circumstances aligned with that state. Songs with positive lyrics and upbeat rhythms vibrate at the frequencies of joy, gratitude, and growth. On the other hand, soft and relaxing melodies align with the vibrations of peace, harmony, and balance. Thus, the conscious selection of music not only influences mood but can also transform our reality by attracting energies that drive our goals.

Several musical styles are especially effective in raising vibration and attracting abundance. Classical music, for example, has been valued for centuries for its harmonious and complex compositions. Works by Mozart, Bach, and Beethoven carry high frequencies that promote mental clarity, emotional balance, and serenity. Listening to a symphony or a piano concerto can awaken creativity and stimulate focus, providing an internal environment conducive to the manifestation of desires. These songs not only enchant the senses but also act as stimuli for the expansion of mind and spirit.

Instrumental music, in turn, offers a pure and welcoming sound experience. Without the influence of words, melodies created by instruments such as piano, violin, flute, and harp calm the mind and reduce stress, amplifying the connection with the energy of abundance. These sounds are ideal for moments of introspection, meditation, or study, creating a serene vibrational space conducive to the flow of ideas and positive feelings. The soft sound of a harp or the delicate notes of a piano can dissolve tensions and open the way to a feeling of peace and fulfillment.

Mantras are another powerful resource. Composed of sacred sounds repeated continuously, mantras carry frequencies capable of silencing the mind and aligning the body's energies. The simple sound "Om" or mantras in Sanskrit activate energy centers and create an atmosphere of introspection and spiritual connection. Integrating mantras into your daily routine is an effective way to tune in to high frequencies, facilitating the manifestation of prosperity and well-being. By repeating these sounds, we create a vibrational field that strengthens the mind and calms the spirit.

In addition, music with inspiring lyrics and positive messages has the power to nourish the mind with constructive thoughts. Songs that talk about self-love, overcoming, and achievements reinforce beliefs that favor the flow of abundance. By listening to or singing these songs, we internalize their messages, raising our vibration and creating an internal environment favorable to success. The energy of these songs stimulates confidence and motivation, directly influencing the way we face challenges and pursue our goals.

The sounds of nature also play a fundamental role in energy harmonization. The sound of the waves of the sea, the singing of birds, or the softness of the rain evoke the connection with the natural cycle of life. These natural vibrations promote deep relaxation and energy renewal, helping to calm the mind and restore emotional balance. Incorporating these sounds into everyday life, whether through recordings or direct experiences, is a way to reconnect with the essence of nature and absorb its vital energy.

To enhance the impact of music on the manifestation of abundance, it is essential to listen to it with intention. Before starting a song, take a moment to close your eyes, breathe deeply, and set a clear intention. Visualize what you want to attract and allow the sound vibrations to align your energies with that purpose. This simple gesture transforms the experience of listening to music into a powerful manifestation exercise, where each note acts as a channel to materialize your desires.

Singing along with the music also amplifies its vibrations. By vocalizing positive lyrics with enthusiasm, you integrate the energy of the music into your vibrational field. It doesn't matter the vocal technique or the tuning, but the authenticity and emotion transmitted. This act of expression releases emotions, dissolves blockages, and reinforces the attunement with prosperity. Allowing yourself to sing freely is to open space for energy to flow and strengthen the connection with your goals.

Dancing to the sound of music is another form of energy integration. The movement of the body in tune with the melody helps to release tensions and emotional blocks. Spontaneous dance, without rules or predefined steps, allows the body to express itself freely, creating a continuous flow of positive energy. This natural movement strengthens the harmony between body, mind, and spirit, enhancing the attraction of abundance in a light and pleasurable way.

Creating an abundance playlist is a simple but very effective practice. Select songs that evoke joy, gratitude, and prosperity. Include tracks with inspiring lyrics, vibrant melodies, and rhythms that motivate you. Listening to this playlist daily, especially when starting the day or during moments of creation, helps keep your vibration high and aligned with your goals. This personalized music selection becomes a constant source of inspiration and energy alignment.

Integrating music into manifestation rituals also enhances results. During creative visualization practices, positive affirmations, or meditations, choose soundtracks that reinforce your intention. Music creates an emotionally engaging environment, making these moments deeper and more effective. This sound support amplifies the connection with your desires, facilitating the materialization of dreams and goals.

Finally, sharing music with loved ones amplifies positive energy. Sharing songs that inspire you strengthens emotional bonds and creates moments of connection and joy. Music, as a universal language, unites people and spreads high vibrations. Organizing musical gatherings or simply sending a meaningful song can be a powerful gesture to nurture relationships and expand the energy of abundance in your social circle.

By understanding music as a tool for transformation, we begin to use it more consciously and strategically. Each note carries the power to shape emotions, unlock energies, and align intentions with what we want to manifest. Incorporating these sounds into moments of introspection, celebration, or simple relaxation connects us with a continuous flow of well-being, creativity, and prosperity. Thus, music becomes a link between the material and spiritual worlds, leading us with lightness and purpose towards a full and abundant life.

When we understand music as a tool for transformation, we begin to use it more consciously and strategically in our journey of self-knowledge and evolution. Each note, each beat, carries with it the power to shape emotions, unlock energies, and align intentions with what we want to manifest. By exploring sounds that resonate with our goals and emotional states, we create an internal environment conducive to the flourishing of creativity, emotional health, and prosperity. Thus, music becomes a link between the material and spiritual worlds, gently guiding us towards a fuller and more harmonious life.

This sound integration does not require great rituals or radical changes in routine; small gestures, such as listening to a calm melody upon waking or choosing an inspiring song during work, can generate significant impacts. The key is the intention with which we connect to these sounds and the sensitivity to perceive how they affect our vibration. By making music a constant ally, we develop the ability to recalibrate our energies in the face of daily challenges, nurturing a more open, resilient, and aligned mindset with the natural flow of abundance.

Therefore, cultivating a conscious relationship with music is allowing yourself to navigate with more lightness and purpose through the ups and downs of life. Whether through sounds of nature that soothe, mantras that uplift the spirit, or vibrant rhythms that awaken motivation, music offers endless possibilities for healing and expansion. By making room for these frequencies in our daily lives, we not only beautify our days but also create a solid foundation for living with more balance, joy, and fulfillment.

Chapter 16
Meditation for Abundance

Meditation is a powerful and accessible tool that allows you to cultivate abundance consciously and profoundly. Through inner silence and connection with the present moment, this practice strengthens the ability to align thoughts, emotions, and actions with the energy of prosperity. By dedicating daily moments to quiet the mind and nurture inner peace, a space conducive to the flow of opportunities and achievements is created. This state of balance facilitates the recognition of paths that lead to personal, financial, and spiritual growth, allowing abundance to manifest naturally and constantly.

By integrating meditation into your routine, you develop a clearer perception of goals and desires, eliminating limiting beliefs and negative thought patterns. This mental clarity opens doors to more assertive choices, strengthening confidence in one's own journey and connection to essential internal resources for success. With a calm mind and an open heart, it is possible to perceive more clearly the opportunities that arise, in addition to maintaining focus and motivation to transform intentions into concrete results. This inner alignment creates a magnetic field favorable to the achievement of goals and the attainment of a full and prosperous life.

In addition to providing emotional balance, meditation also enhances creativity, intuition, and resilience. These aspects are fundamental to facing challenges and adapting to new circumstances with wisdom and confidence. Cultivating this state of mindful presence allows access to innovative solutions and unexplored paths, facilitating the construction of a reality aligned with dreams and goals. Thus, meditative practice becomes a bridge between the desire to prosper and the realization of an abundant existence, sustained by well-being, harmony, and personal fulfillment.

Imagine a lake of crystalline waters. When its surface is agitated by winds and waves, it becomes impossible to see the bottom. But when the waters calm down, the hidden beauty is revealed: the stones, the fish, and the serene depth. So is the human mind. Meditation works like this process of calming the inner waters, silencing the agitation of thoughts and allowing access to clarity, inner peace, and connection with the abundance that resides within us. In this state of stillness, it is possible to clearly perceive the paths that lead to personal, financial, and spiritual growth, opening space for opportunities to flow freely.

When we meditate, we enter a state of receptivity that aligns us with the frequency of what we want to manifest. Constant practice puts us in harmony with the energy of abundance, making us open channels for it to manifest in all areas of life. During meditation, visualizing dreams come true, repeating positive affirmations, or simply feeling gratitude for what we already have strengthens the connection with prosperity. This vibrational alignment enhances the materialization of goals and transforms desires into reality.

Among the most notable benefits of meditation is the reduction of stress and anxiety. Excessive worry blocks the natural flow of abundance, creating mental and emotional resistance. Meditative practice significantly reduces levels of cortisol, the stress hormone, promoting emotional balance and a lighter, clearer mind. This state of inner calm not only improves well-being, but also facilitates the recognition of new opportunities and opens space for more accurate decision-making.

Meditation is also a powerful ally to increase focus and concentration. When the mind is freed from the scattering of thoughts, it becomes easier to maintain full attention in the present and direct mental energy towards concrete goals. This clarity is essential for defining goals, outlining strategies, and persisting in projects with discipline. With improved focus, decisions become more assertive, and the path to prosperity becomes clearer.

Another essential aspect of meditation is the raising of energy vibration. By entering deep states of serenity, the vibrational frequency of the body and mind rises, attracting experiences and people aligned with the energy of prosperity. The higher this vibration, the easier it becomes to materialize goals. This high-frequency state creates a powerful magnetic field where positive thoughts and clear intentions flow towards the realization of dreams.

Furthermore, meditative practice releases creative flow. In inner silence, new ideas and innovative solutions arise naturally, favoring the creation of projects and the development of strategies that drive success. This creativity is not limited to artistic activities but extends to problem-solving and identifying unexplored paths. The open and calm mind is fertile ground for innovation, an essential factor in achieving prosperity.

Meditation also deepens the connection with intuition. This inner guide, often muffled by the noise of thoughts, becomes more accessible when the mind is calm. Important decisions are made with more confidence, as intuition points the way that is most aligned with goals. Trusting your instincts strengthens decision-making and opens space to recognize previously invisible opportunities.

On the physical aspect, meditation promotes health and vitality. Studies show that regular practice reduces blood pressure, improves blood circulation, and strengthens the immune system. A healthy body supports a balanced mind, and this integral harmony creates the ideal foundation for the energy of abundance to flow without blockages. Taking care of physical and mental well-being is essential to maintain the balance needed to thrive.

Various meditation techniques can be incorporated to attract abundance. Gratitude Meditation is one of the most effective. In a quiet environment, simply close your eyes and focus on your breathing. Gradually bring to mind people, situations, and achievements for which you are grateful. Feel gratitude expand, enveloping your entire being like a soft light. This energy creates a cycle of recognition and attraction of new blessings.

Another powerful practice is Visualization Meditation. In it, we visualize in detail the goals already achieved. Imagine yourself living the life you want, feel the emotions of satisfaction and see the environments around you. The more vivid the visualization, the stronger the link with the frequency of abundance. This technique inspires concrete and targeted actions to materialize dreams.

Meditation with Affirmations also enhances the connection with prosperity. Choose phrases like "I am worthy of a prosperous life" or "Abundance flows freely to me" and repeat them with conviction. Feeling the power of each word is essential to dissolve limiting beliefs and create new mental programs. The constant repetition of these affirmations reinforces self-confidence and strengthens the path to success.

For those seeking guidance, Guided Meditation is an excellent option. Guided by a soft voice and accompanied by relaxing music, this practice leads to deep states of relaxation and connection. During meditation, we are invited to visualize scenarios of success, peace, and prosperity. This process helps the subconscious mind absorb the intentions of abundance and manifest them in reality.

Meditation with Mantras is also effective in raising energy vibration. Sitting comfortably, choose a powerful mantra, such as "Om Shreem Maha Lakshmiyei Namaha" or "I am abundance". Inhale deeply and chant the mantra, feeling its vibration travel through your body. Repetition creates a flow of energy that dissolves blockages and strengthens attunement with prosperity.

For meditation to be effective, it is important to create a conducive environment. Choose a quiet place where you can relax without interruption. A special corner of the house, decorated with candles, cushions, and soft scents, becomes a sacred space for practice. Adopting a comfortable posture, with an upright spine and relaxed body, facilitates the flow of energy. Focus on your breathing, watching the air naturally enter and exit, and allow thoughts to pass without attachment or judgment.

It is essential to cultivate patience and persistence. Meditation is a continuous journey of self-knowledge and transformation. There is no need for haste or pressure. Each practice, however brief, contributes to strengthening the connection with abundance. Consistency transforms small moments of silence into a powerful lever for a full life.

Incorporating meditation into your daily routine transforms not only the mind but also the way we see the world. This silent process strengthens self-confidence and dissolves internal resistance. With each conscious breath, we come closer to understanding that prosperity begins within us and is reflected in every choice and action. This balance between body, mind, and spirit creates fertile ground for the materialization of our dreams.

By persisting in meditative practice, you build a reality based on abundance, where desires are transformed into achievements and challenges are learning opportunities. Meditation, therefore, is not just a refuge, but an inexhaustible source of strength and inspiration to live with purpose, balance, and fulfillment.

By incorporating meditation as a daily habit, you gradually transform your perception of yourself and the world around you. This silent and profound process strengthens inner confidence and dissolves resistances that once seemed insurmountable. With each conscious breath, you approach a reality where abundance is not just a distant ideal, but a natural expression of your essence. With an open mind and a receptive heart, you begin to recognize that prosperity starts from the inside out, reflecting in every aspect of your life.

This journey of self-knowledge reveals that abundance is directly linked to the balance between body, mind, and spirit. When you take care of your integral well-being, you create fertile ground for ideas to flourish, decisions to be made wisely, and opportunities to be embraced with confidence. Meditation not only calms the mind but also expands consciousness, allowing you to understand that you are deserving of all forms of prosperity. This state of inner harmony drives your actions, making the path to success clearer and more accessible.

Thus, by persisting in meditative practice and nurturing positive thoughts, you build a reality based on abundance and fullness. Each moment of silence becomes an opportunity for alignment with the natural flow of the universe, where dreams are transformed into achievements and challenges are converted into learning. Meditation, therefore, is not just a refuge, but an inexhaustible source of strength, clarity, and inspiration to live abundantly and meaningfully.

Chapter 17
Powerful Mantras

Mantras are powerful instruments of transformation that channel positive energies and raise the vibrational frequency of those who practice them. Each sound, word or phrase in Sanskrit carries a specific energetic charge, capable of profoundly influencing the body, mind and spirit. The regular practice of these sacred chants establishes a direct connection with universal forces, activating internal energy centers and unlocking paths to well-being and prosperity.

The vibration generated by a mantra acts in a subtle and effective way, harmonizing thoughts, emotions and intentions, creating an environment conducive to the manifestation of desires and goals. Thus, the conscious and dedicated use of mantras becomes a bridge between the inner world and external opportunities, promoting balance, clarity and personal transformation.

By chanting a mantra with full attention, the mind becomes still and vital energy flows more freely, dissolving internal and external barriers. This practice requires not only mechanical repetition, but also total presence and the clear intention to align oneself with the desired purpose. The generated sound vibration resonates deeply in the body, stimulating energy centers, such as the chakras, and promoting a sense of peace and expansion. This experience not only calms the mental flow, but also awakens a state of receptivity and openness to new possibilities, attracting opportunities, people and circumstances that vibrate at the same frequency as the cultivated intention. In this way, mantras become essential allies for those seeking personal growth, emotional balance and abundance in all areas of life.

Integrating the practice of mantras into your daily routine is an effective way to strengthen your connection with your own inner power and with universal forces. Consciously choosing the mantra that most resonates with your goals amplifies the strength of intention and enhances results. Regularity in chanting and sincere devotion intensify the energy emanated, creating a solid foundation for the manifestation of dreams and projects. Thus, each recited word becomes a vibrational seed planted in the energy field, ready to flourish in the form of concrete achievements. This continuous process of alignment and expansion strengthens self-confidence and cultivates a lasting sense of peace, prosperity and personal fulfillment.

Imagine a mantra as a key capable of opening invisible doors, allowing the energy of the universe to flow freely into your life. Each sacred sound carries a unique vibration that resonates with distinct aspects of existence, activating energy centers, calming the mind and creating paths for the realization of dreams. Just as a melody can deeply touch the soul, a mantra chanted with clear intention and total presence acts as a silent guide, leading you to higher states of consciousness and aligning your energy with the frequency of abundance.

The constant practice of mantras is an effective way to raise personal vibration. When we repeat sacred sounds with devotion, we create an energetic resonance capable of harmonizing body, mind and spirit. This alignment strengthens the connection with higher forces and puts us in tune with opportunities, people and circumstances that vibrate at the same frequency as our desires. Thus, chanting mantras is not just a vocal exercise, but a practice of deep inner transformation that expands our perception and makes us receptive to prosperity.

Among the most powerful mantras to attract abundance is Om Gam Ganapataye Namaha, an invocation to the energy of Ganesha, the remover of obstacles. This mantra strengthens the ability to overcome challenges, unlock paths and create an environment favorable to success. By chanting it with faith, space is opened for new opportunities and achievements, allowing energy to flow more freely in personal and professional projects.

Another essential mantra is Om Shrim Maha Lakshmyai Namaha, which connects directly to the goddess Lakshmi, a symbol of prosperity and abundance. Its constant repetition not only attracts material wealth, but also promotes financial balance and well-being. This mantra cultivates an energy of fullness, where luck and harmony flow naturally, filling life with prosperity on several levels.

For those seeking creative fertility and growth in various areas, Om Vasudhare Svaha is a powerful connection to the goddess Vasudhara. This mantra stimulates the expansion of ideas and projects, fertilizing the ground for the flourishing of new opportunities. Its regular practice promotes material abundance, spiritual balance and innovation, creating ideal conditions for achieving goals.

Om Kubera Lakshmi Namah unites the forces of Kubera, god of wealth, and Lakshmi, goddess of prosperity, enhancing the attraction of material gains and business success. By reciting this mantra, financial flows are unlocked, strategic vision is expanded and the economic base is strengthened, creating stability and continuous growth.

Om Namah Shivaya is one of the most powerful mantras for personal transformation. Reverencing Shiva, the god of destruction and renewal, it dissolves mental and emotional blocks, freeing vital energy. Its practice encourages the courage to change and opens space for abundance to flow freely and naturally, promoting spiritual evolution and personal fulfillment.

To fully enjoy the benefits of these mantras, it is essential to practice them with presence and intention. The first step is to choose the mantra that most resonates with your goals. Let your intuition guide this choice, feeling which sound awakens a genuine connection with what you want to manifest. Then find a quiet environment, free from distractions, where you can sit comfortably. Preparing this space with candles, incense or symbolic objects can help create an atmosphere of concentration and harmony.

Before starting the repetition, focus on your breathing. Inhale deeply through your nose and exhale slowly through your mouth, allowing your body to relax and your mind to become still. This breathing preparation is essential to truly connect with the vibration of the mantra. Begin chanting it aloud, whispering or mentally, feeling the resonance of each sound fill your being. A japamala (rosary of 108 beads) can be used to keep track of repetitions and maintain focus.

While reciting, visualize your goals already achieved. Imagine the details, feel the emotions of accomplishment and allow this visualization to involve your entire energy field. The more vivid this experience, the more powerful the manifestation will be. Let the vibration of the mantra run through your body, expanding and harmonizing your energies, creating a deep connection with the universal flow of prosperity.

Constant practice is fundamental. Incorporating mantras into your daily routine strengthens your connection to the invoked energy. Regular repetition intensifies the effects, creating a solid and lasting vibrational field. Whether in the morning, to start the day with focus and clarity, or before bed, to calm the mind and program the subconscious, consistency brings deeper and more effective results.

Some tips can further enhance this practice. Correctly pronouncing each syllable of the mantra is essential, as each sound carries a specific vibration.

Seeking guidance from authentic recordings or reliable sources ensures that the energy of the mantra is fully activated. Furthermore, intention is the foundation of practice. Focus deeply on the purpose you want to achieve, channeling thoughts and emotions towards that goal.

Full concentration during chanting keeps the mind focused, keeping distractions away. This deep meditative state strengthens the spiritual connection and enhances the benefits of the mantra. True devotion, performed with respect and gratitude, intensifies this connection with sacred energies. Each repetition becomes an offering of faith, deepening the spiritual experience.

Over time, the dedicated practice of mantras becomes a path of self-knowledge and expansion of consciousness. Constant repetition not only strengthens the connection with higher energies, but also reveals hidden potentials, awakening dormant talents. This gradual process dissolves limiting patterns, allowing for a more positive and broader view of life. Mantras cease to be just tools of manifestation and become instruments of spiritual evolution and emotional balance.

Furthermore, the journey with mantras teaches the importance of patience and surrender. Results are not always immediate, but each repetition plants a seed that grows silently. Continuous practice develops trust in the flow of life, allowing challenges to be seen as learning opportunities. This conscious surrender opens space for synchronicities, where events align perfectly with desires and goals, reinforcing faith in the power of sacred words.

By integrating mantras into your routine, you create a continuous cycle of renewal and balance. Each chanted sound reverberates not only in the body and mind, but also transforms the environment, making it lighter, more harmonious and prosperous. Thus, mantras are consolidated as powerful allies in the journey of personal transformation, guiding the practitioner towards a more conscious life, fulfilled and in perfect harmony with the universe.

Over time, the dedicated practice of mantras becomes a true path of self-knowledge and expansion of consciousness. Constant repetition not only strengthens the connection with higher energies, but also deepens the understanding of oneself, revealing hidden potentials and awakening dormant talents. This gradual process allows the practitioner to free himself from limiting patterns and develop a broader and more positive view of life, aligning himself with the natural flow of the universe. Thus, mantras become not only tools of manifestation, but also instruments of spiritual evolution and emotional balance.

Furthermore, the journey with mantras teaches the importance of patience and surrender. Results are not always immediate, but each repetition plants a seed that grows silently, shaping reality according to the intention sown. Continuous practice brings a sense of trust in the process of life, allowing the practitioner to embrace challenges as opportunities for growth. This conscious surrender opens space for synchronicity, where seemingly random events align perfectly with the desires and goals cultivated, reinforcing faith in the power of sacred words.

By integrating mantras as an essential part of the routine, a constant cycle of renewal and balance is created. Each chanted sound reverberates not only in the body and mind, but also in the surrounding environment, transforming everyday life into a lighter, more harmonious and prosperous space. This continuous practice establishes a solid foundation for building a full life, where abundance flows naturally and challenges are faced with wisdom and serenity. Thus, mantras are consolidated as powerful allies in the journey of personal transformation, guiding the practitioner towards a more conscious existence, fulfilled and in perfect harmony with the universe.

Chapter 18
Sacred Mudras

Mudras are powerful hand gestures that act directly on the harmonization of vital energy (prana), promoting physical, mental and spiritual balance. Its millennial practice in traditions such as yoga and meditation reveals a deep knowledge about the connection between body and energy, being able to unblock energy flows, activate chakras and enhance states of well-being and abundance. Each gesture carries a specific meaning, functioning as a direct channel to manifest prosperity, health, love and inner peace. By practicing mudras with clear intention and full awareness, a bridge is created between the inner world and universal forces, allowing energy to flow freely and align the being with its deepest goals.

The hands, when positioned precisely in mudras, become effective instruments for directing and amplifying the subtle energy that circulates through the body. This process strengthens the connection with one's own essence and with the surrounding energy field, dissolving blockages and awakening latent potentials. The regular practice of mudras not only nourishes physical vitality, but also expands emotional and spiritual perception, creating a solid foundation for transforming thoughts and feelings into concrete actions. This harmonious integration between intention and energy enhances the manifestation of positive results, allowing the construction of a more balanced and prosperous reality.

By adopting mudras as part of your daily routine, you establish a continuous path of self-knowledge and inner strengthening. The simple act of consciously positioning your fingers activates energy centers that support health, emotional balance and mental clarity. Thus, each gesture becomes a practical tool to reconnect with the natural abundance of the universe, promoting a fuller life aligned with higher purposes.

Imagine your hands as channels of energy, capable of capturing and directing subtle forces that circulate through the body and the universe. When we form mudras with awareness and intention, these gestures become powerful tools of connection between the inner world and the universal flow of abundance, health, love and peace. Each finger position is like a circuit that closes, conducting prana - vital energy - to specific areas of the body and mind, awakening latent potentials and dissolving energy blocks.

In the practice of yoga and meditation, mudras are used to balance the chakras and regulate the flow of prana, creating physical, mental and spiritual harmony. By activating these energy centers, internal tensions are removed and space is opened for the energy of abundance to flow freely. This balance between body, mind and spirit establishes a solid foundation for the manifestation of prosperity and well-being in all areas of life. Thus, mudras are not just symbolic gestures, but practical instruments to align oneself with the natural flow of the universe.

Among the most effective mudras to attract abundance, Kubera Mudra stands out, inspired by Kubera, the Hindu god of wealth and prosperity. This gesture is simple, but powerful: the tips of the thumb, index and middle fingers are joined, while the ring and little fingers remain folded towards the palm. This position activates the solar plexus chakra, responsible for personal power and self-confidence, concentrating intention and directing energy towards the achievement of material goals. With regular practice, Kubera Mudra strengthens determination and attracts opportunities for success.

Another gesture of great power is Lakshmi Mudra, which invokes the energy of the goddess Lakshmi, a symbol of abundance and prosperity. To perform it, position your hands with your palms facing up and join the tips of your thumbs, keeping your other fingers extended and relaxed. This gesture activates the heart chakra, expanding feelings of love, gratitude and compassion. Opening the heart creates a continuous flow of positive energy, facilitating the reception of material and emotional prosperity. Lakshmi Mudra not only attracts external wealth, but also nourishes inner well-being.

Varuna Mudra is ideal for those looking to unblock repressed emotions and stimulate creativity. Dedicated to Varuna, the god of water, this mudra balances the water element in the body and activates the sacral chakra, linked to emotional fluidity and creative expression. To practice it, simply join the tip of the little finger with the tip of the thumb, leaving the other fingers relaxed. This gesture promotes the release of accumulated feelings, bringing lightness and adaptability in the face of changes, which facilitates the natural flow of abundance in different areas of life.

Prithvi Mudra is a gesture that strengthens stability and grounding, essential for attracting lasting prosperity. Inspired by Prithvi, the earth goddess, it activates the root chakra, responsible for security and connection to the physical world. To perform it, join the tip of the ring finger with the tip of the thumb, keeping the other fingers extended. This gesture increases the feeling of firmness, balances the physical and mental body and reinforces confidence, creating a solid foundation for material and spiritual growth.

For energy purification and renewal, Apana Mudra is a powerful tool. It helps in eliminating physical and emotional toxins, clearing blockages that prevent the free flow of vital energy. To perform it, join the tips of the thumb, middle finger and ring finger, leaving the index and little fingers extended. This gesture activates the natural detoxification process, opening space for renewal and facilitating the manifestation of new cycles of abundance and balance.

To enhance the effects of mudras, it is important to practice them consciously. Start by choosing the mudra that most resonates with your goals. Trust your intuition to identify which gesture aligns with your desires, whether it be attracting prosperity, achieving emotional balance or promoting healing. After this choice, find a calm environment, free from distractions, where you can sit or stay comfortable. A quiet place, harmonized with candles, scents or soft light, helps to create an atmosphere conducive to practice.

Focus on your breathing. Breathe in deeply, feeling the air fill your body, and exhale slowly, releasing tension. Conscious breathing relaxes the body and calms the mind, creating the ideal state to fully absorb the benefits of mudra. With your body relaxed, form the chosen gesture, positioning your fingers precisely. Keep your posture upright, but without stiffness, allowing energy to flow freely.

While holding the mudra, visualize your goals already achieved. Imagine the details clearly, feel the emotion of having achieved what you want. This visualization strengthens the connection between your intention and the energy you are channeling. Notice the sensations that arise: warmth, tingling or lightness in your hands and body. These perceptions indicate that the energy flow has been activated. Allow this positive vibration to expand, harmonizing your energy field.

Regular practice of mudras enhances its effects. Dedicate a few minutes each day to this connection. Consistency strengthens energy alignment and intensifies the desired results. Incorporating mudras into your daily routine creates a cycle of renewal and balance, sustaining harmony between body, mind and spirit.

Some practices can further deepen the experience. Set a clear intention before starting. Know exactly what you want to attract, be it prosperity, peace or balance. Direct all your attention to the gesture and breathing, keeping distracting thoughts away. Stay relaxed, without muscle tension, and synchronize the practice with deep, conscious breathing. Observe the sensations during the exercise and trust this natural flow of energy.

Over time, the continuous practice of mudras reveals its transformative power. Each conscious gesture expands the connection with the universal flow, allowing abundance and balance to flow naturally in everyday life. This process awakens dormant potentials and dissolves blockages that prevented growth. The energy that was previously dispersed begins to be channeled with clarity and purpose, creating conditions for a fuller life aligned with the true desires of the soul.

Thus, mudras become silent but deeply effective allies in the journey of self-knowledge and evolution. Incorporating them into your routine is opening yourself to a constant flow of balance, healing and prosperity. May each gesture be an invitation to dive deeper into yourself, awakening your inner power and allowing the energy of the universe to flow freely, leading you to an existence full of purpose, harmony and fulfillment.

With the continuous practice of mudras, it becomes evident that these simple gestures carry a profound wisdom, capable of transforming not only emotional and mental states, but also the very reality around them. Each conscious movement of the hands strengthens the connection with the universal flow of energy, allowing abundance and balance to become natural experiences in everyday life. The integration of these practices into the routine reveals paths of self-discovery and empowerment, where the harmony between intention and action manifests positive and lasting changes.

By recognizing the strength of mudras as instruments of transformation, the perception of one's own inner power is expanded. The energy that previously flowed in a dispersed way begins to be channeled with clarity and purpose, awakening dormant potentialities. This intimate connection with vital energy inspires a journey of constant growth, where each gesture, each breath and each thought collaborate to build a fuller, more conscious life aligned with the true desires of the soul.

Thus, mudras are revealed as silent but powerful allies on the path of personal evolution. Incorporating these sacred gestures into everyday life is allowing yourself to access an inexhaustible source of balance, healing and prosperity. May each practice be an invitation to delve deeper into self-knowledge, opening space for the energy of the universe to flow freely and lead the being to an existence full of purpose, peace and fulfillment.

Chapter 19
Dance and Movement

Dance represents an authentic and profound expression of human essence, capable of unlocking energies, revitalizing the body, and connecting the mind to the natural flow of the universe. Through free movement, the body transforms into a channel of expression that releases accumulated tensions and promotes a state of physical, emotional, and spiritual balance. This intimate connection with one's own rhythm and with music creates a space where vital energy circulates without impediments, providing well-being, lightness, and fullness. Dance, thus, transcends the simple act of moving, becoming a powerful practice of self-knowledge and reconnection with one's own essence, facilitating the manifestation of abundance in various aspects of life.

By allowing the body to move spontaneously, each gesture becomes an act of freedom, dissolving emotional and mental barriers that limit creative potential and the ability to attract prosperity. This natural movement not only strengthens physical health, but also opens space for feelings of joy, confidence, and inner renewal. The continuous flow of energy released by dance revitalizes the body, clears the mind, and balances emotions, creating fertile ground for the flourishing of new opportunities and achievements. In this way, dance presents itself as a bridge between the body and the mind, aligning both with the dynamic rhythm of life.

Incorporating dance into everyday life is allowing yourself to fully experience your own existence, honoring the body as an instrument of expression and manifestation of desires and intentions. Each step and conscious movement expands the connection with the present and strengthens confidence in one's own abilities, awakening creativity and nurturing vitality. This deep involvement with dance not only provides moments of pleasure and fun, but also contributes directly to building a more abundant, healthy, and harmonious life. Thus, moving freely is also moving the energy of life, attracting prosperity and happiness in a natural and fluid way.

Imagine dance as a true ritual of celebrating life, where each movement becomes a tribute to the body, soul, and creative energy that pulsates within you. By surrendering to the rhythm of the music, your body transforms into an open channel for the manifestation of abundance. Each step taken, each spontaneous turn, and each natural sway are invitations for prosperity, health, and happiness to approach, flowing smoothly into your existence. It is not just about moving, but about feeling dance as a bridge between your inner being and the subtle forces of the universe, where vital energy circulates freely, dissolving blockages and creating space for new possibilities.

In this context, dance is revealed as a moving meditation. Each gesture performed spontaneously allows you to connect deeply with the present moment. The accumulated stress, daily tensions, and worries that once weighed on your shoulders gradually melt away, freeing up space for authentic and liberating expression. The body, now loose and free, becomes the conductor of vital energy, flowing without resistance and dissipating obstacles that previously limited the path to abundance. This state of full presence opens doors to a meaningful experience, where movement is not only physical, but also emotional and spiritual.

By allowing yourself to dance with total surrender, you begin a profound process of emotional release. Dance becomes a safe vehicle for expressing repressed feelings, functioning as an escape valve for emotions that are often ignored or kept. Laughing, crying, or even screaming during the dance are natural expressions that promote emotional healing, dissolving inner tensions and creating space for lighter and more positive emotions to settle in. This emotional freedom is essential to cultivate a balanced mind and an open heart, fundamental conditions for abundance to flourish.

The physical benefits of dance are equally remarkable. Constant movement stimulates blood circulation and improves oxygenation of the body, revitalizing the body from the inside out. This renewed flow of energy strengthens the immune system and increases physical disposition, making the body more resilient and healthy. The feeling of increasing vitality directly reflects in the way you face life, with more enthusiasm and courage to face challenges and embrace opportunities.

Furthermore, dance deepens the connection with one's own body. With each movement, you become more aware of your sensations, rhythms, and limits, developing a keen body perception. This physical self-knowledge not only strengthens the relationship with your essence, but also creates a solid foundation for self-confidence. Feeling comfortable in your own body is a crucial step in accepting who you are, valuing your uniqueness and recognizing your own worth. This reinforced self-esteem is reflected in a more positive attitude towards life, directly influencing interpersonal relationships and the way you deal with the world around you.

Dance is also a powerful source of creativity. Free and spontaneous movements break with rigid patterns, stimulating the emergence of new ideas and creative solutions. This creative flow is not limited to the body, but extends to various areas of life, enhancing intuition and the ability to face challenges in innovative ways. Each improvisation in dance is a reflection of the ability to adapt and find new paths, valuable skills to achieve prosperity in all spheres of existence.

Another significant impact of dance is stress reduction. The simple act of moving to music stimulates the release of endorphins, hormones responsible for the feeling of pleasure and well-being. This natural chemical response relieves tension, reduces anxiety, and promotes a state of inner calm. By integrating this practice regularly, you create a more stable and resilient emotional foundation that favors the balance needed to attract and sustain abundance in your life.

The lightness and spontaneity awakened by dance also strengthen the connection with genuine joy. Unpretentious and free movements awaken feelings of fun and contentment, raising your energetic vibration. This elevated state of vibration acts as a magnet for positive experiences, bringing prosperity, health, and happiness closer. The joy felt during the dance resonates beyond the present moment, influencing your attitude towards life and opening doors to new opportunities.

To fully enjoy these benefits, it is essential to create an environment conducive to dancing. Choose a comfortable and quiet space where you can move freely and without distractions. A harmonious environment, with soft lighting, pleasant aromas and inspiring elements, such as plants or meaningful objects, contributes to your energy flowing naturally. This safe and welcoming space facilitates connection with the present moment, allowing you to fully immerse yourself in the experience.

Music plays a fundamental role in this process. Select melodies that evoke positive emotions and bring lightness to your heart. Whether it's soft music, nature sounds, or vibrant rhythms, the important thing is that the sound resonates with your energy at that moment. Closing your eyes while dancing can further deepen this connection, eliminating distractions and allowing each note and beat to guide your movements authentically.

Allow your body to respond naturally to the music, without worrying about correct steps or rhythm.

Smooth or intense movements should arise spontaneously, respecting your own time and desires. This bodily freedom dissolves inner blockages and creates a continuous flow of energy, opening space for abundance to manifest. If you feel like expressing intense emotions, such as laughing or crying, embrace these feelings without restriction. This emotional surrender strengthens inner healing and expands the capacity to feel lightness and positivity.

While dancing, visualize your goals already achieved. Imagine in detail the achievements you want to achieve, feeling the satisfaction and joy of already having these desires fulfilled. This practice of visualization, aligned with movement, enhances the connection with the energy of abundance, guiding thoughts, emotions and actions towards your dreams.

At the end of the dance, take a moment to give thanks. Acknowledge the achievements that are already part of your life and express gratitude for the opportunities that are to come. This simple gesture strengthens your positive vibration and keeps the connection to prosperity open. Gratitude is a powerful key that expands the ability to attract and sustain abundance.

Free yourself from judgments and embrace dance as a genuine form of expression. Don't seek perfection or ideal technique. Just move, feel the music and let each gesture reveal who you are. Celebrate each movement as an act of freedom, fun and connection with life. In this natural flow, dance becomes a powerful ally on the journey to a full, abundant and purposeful existence.

By integrating dance as a natural part of your routine, you cultivate a more intimate relationship with your own body and with the energy that moves it. This commitment to yourself does not require great performances or elaborate techniques, but rather authenticity and surrender to the moment. Small daily gestures, such as swaying your body to the sound of soft music or allowing spontaneous movements while performing simple tasks, are enough to keep the energy flow active. This constant practice strengthens the connection with inner vitality, allowing abundance to manifest organically in all aspects of life.

Over time, this spontaneous bodily expression transforms not only the body, but also the perception of challenges and opportunities. The mind becomes lighter and more open, favoring more creative decisions that are aligned with true desires. Self-confidence gains new dimensions, driving the search for enriching experiences and more authentic relationships. Dance, in this context, ceases to be a simple physical act and becomes a true dialogue between being and the universe, where each movement is an invitation for prosperity and harmony to establish themselves naturally.

Thus, by allowing yourself to dance freely, you activate a positive cycle of renewal and growth. The fluidity of movements symbolizes flexibility in the face of life, teaching the importance of adapting and flowing with changes. In this continuous rhythm between body, mind and spirit, dance is revealed as a powerful path to awaken the unlimited potential that exists within each one. And it is in this compass of freedom and connection that abundance finds space to flourish, guiding you to a full journey of balance, health and fulfillment.

Chapter 20
Energy Baths

Energy baths play a fundamental role in harmonizing the body, mind and spirit, functioning as a powerful tool for cleansing and revitalizing energy. Just as the physical body needs regular care to stay healthy, the energy field also demands practices that promote balance and well-being. Through the combination of natural elements, such as herbs, flowers and crystals, these baths act directly on the removal of negative charges, dissipating emotional and spiritual blockages. By integrating these rituals into everyday life, it becomes possible to release stagnant energies and open space for a fluid circulation of positive vibrations, creating a favorable internal environment for personal and spiritual growth.

Each ingredient used in energy baths carries unique properties that enhance the process of purification and attraction of good energies. Plants such as rue, rosemary and basil are known for their protective and cleansing abilities, while elements such as bay leaf, cinnamon and honey act directly on attracting prosperity and abundance. The conscious choice of these components, combined with clear intention during the preparation and application of the bath, intensifies the desired effect. Thus, these rituals not only cleanse the aura, but also align the chakras and strengthen the vibrational field, creating a protective barrier against negative external influences.

Incorporating energy baths into your routine is an effective way to restore emotional balance, increase vitality and strengthen your connection to the vital energy of the universe. By allowing water impregnated with natural properties to run through the body, a profound renewal takes place that goes beyond the physical aspect, directly influencing the mind and spirit. This purification process not only promotes a feeling of lightness and well-being, but also enhances the ability to attract opportunities, health and happiness. Being in tune with these practices means opening the way to a fuller, more abundant life, aligned with the positive forces that surround everyday life.

Imagine yourself in the midst of nature, in front of a waterfall of crystalline waters that descends in a continuous flow, gently touching your skin. The cold, pure water runs through every part of your body, washing away physical and emotional impurities, while a feeling of renewal takes over you. Just like this natural bath, energy baths act deeply in purifying the aura, balancing the chakras and restoring connection with the vital energy of nature. Each drop of water, impregnated with the healing properties of plants, flowers and crystals, acts as a channel for cleansing and revitalization, dissolving blockages and opening space for positive energy to flow freely.

The aura, this subtle energy field that surrounds the physical body, absorbs external influences daily. Negative emotions, dense thoughts and vibrations from charged environments can accumulate, creating an invisible weight that affects well-being. Energy baths have the ability to remove these dense layers, cleansing and harmonizing the aura. By allowing water mixed with natural elements to run through the skin, there is a release of accumulated tensions, promoting protection and energy balance. This process not only relieves physical fatigue, but also provides emotional lightness and mental clarity.

The purification promoted by these baths directly impacts how abundance manifests itself in life. When the vibrational field is clean and balanced, it becomes easier to attract prosperity, health and happiness. Ingredients such as coarse salt and rue dissolve negative energies, while elements such as bay leaf and honey attract luck and prosperity. The combination of these components, added to the clear intention during the ritual, creates an internal environment conducive to receiving opportunities and living more fully.

In addition to energy cleansing, these baths promote deep emotional balance. Warm water loaded with herbs and flowers envelops the body, calming the mind and heart. Feelings such as anger, sadness or anxiety find an escape valve in this self-care ritual. Ingredients such as chamomile and lavender convey serenity, providing relief and restoring inner peace. This emotional balance not only brings comfort, but also prepares the ground to face challenges with more clarity and lightness.

Vitality is also intensified through energy baths. Physical and mental fatigue dissolves upon contact with water loaded with invigorating properties. Plants such as rosemary and mint awaken inner vigor, increasing disposition and energy for everyday life. This energy renewal strengthens the body and mind, allowing for more efficient performance in all areas of life. Renewed disposition opens space for productivity, creativity and personal and professional growth.

Energy baths also offer powerful protection against negative external influences. Ingredients such as rue and coarse salt create a subtle but effective barrier around the aura, functioning as a shield against envy, the evil eye and charged environments. This energetic shielding prevents harmful vibrations from interfering with your balance, allowing your vibration to remain elevated. This state of continuous protection keeps the mind focused and the heart calm, essential to stay firm in one's own goals.

Another notable benefit is the strengthening of intuition. Energy cleansing undoes mental and emotional blockages, clearing perception and expanding connection with inner wisdom. Ingredients such as white rose and chamomile awaken sensitivity and favor listening to one's own intuition. With the mind free of noise and interference, it becomes easier to make sound decisions and follow paths aligned with your deepest desires. This intuitive clarity guides wiser and more effective choices, enhancing the achievement of goals.

For those seeking to attract prosperity, an energy bath with bay leaves, basil, cinnamon sticks and honey is especially effective. Bay leaf symbolizes success and victory, basil protects and balances, cinnamon intensifies the attraction of good opportunities and honey brings smoothness to the flow of achievements. This preparation, when done with attention and intention, creates a powerful synergy capable of opening paths to abundance. As you pour this infusion over your body, imagine each drop bringing prosperity, filling your life with opportunities and accomplishments.

The energy cleansing bath, with coarse salt, rue and rosemary, offers a deep purification. Salt neutralizes dense charges, rue protects against negative energies and rosemary revitalizes and clears the mind. This ritual dissolves blockages, renews the vibrational field and strengthens energy protection. When performing this bath, visualize all negative influences being dissolved and your body being enveloped by a clear, protective light.

To attract love and harmony, the bath with white rose petals, chamomile flowers and crystal sugar is ideal. The white rose brings peace and purity, chamomile promotes calm and sugar attracts sweetness and good opportunities. When bathing with this infusion, imagine yourself being enveloped by a soft and loving energy, opening yourself to healthy relationships and harmonious experiences.

The effectiveness of these rituals is intensified when performed with full awareness. Before starting the bath, it is essential to establish a clear intention. Take a moment to reflect on what you want to transform or attract into your life. During preparation, handle the ingredients with respect and attention, recognizing the life force that each one carries. This care transforms the bath into a sacred ritual, enhancing its effects.

During the bath, allow yourself to completely relax. Breathe deeply, feeling each tension dissolve. Visualize the water washing away everything that no longer serves you and filling your body with light and positive energy. This visualization practice is a powerful tool that reinforces purification and the attraction of good vibrations.

At the end, take a moment to give thanks. Acknowledge the generosity of nature for the elements used and for the renewal received. This gesture of gratitude expands the connection with natural forces and enhances the effect of the bath. Giving thanks is an act of recognition that creates a cycle of positive energy exchange, opening up even more paths to new blessings.

Thus, by integrating energy baths as part of a conscious routine, a powerful link is created between body, mind and spirit. These moments of self-care become true rituals of reconnection and renewal. With regular practice, not only is the energy field kept clean and protected, but also the mind and heart are strengthened in the face of daily challenges. This energetic balance promotes clarity, serenity and a deep connection with one's own essence.

Over time, these rituals become more than sporadic practices and become a way of life. Each bath is an opportunity for dialogue with the universe, a time to express desires and open paths to fulfillment. In this harmonious flow, vital energy circulates freely, allowing peace, love, health and prosperity to flourish naturally. Thus, each drop of consecrated water becomes a seed of transformation, guiding you towards a full, balanced and abundant life.

By integrating energy baths as part of a conscious ritual, a powerful connection is created between body, mind and spirit, allowing energy to flow harmoniously. More than just a habit, these moments of care become sacred acts of self-compassion and renewal. Regular practice not only keeps the vibrational field clean and protected, but also strengthens the ability to deal with daily challenges with serenity and balance. This energetic alignment brings mental and emotional clarity, facilitating more assertive choices and promoting a lighter and fuller life.

Furthermore, by respecting the time and preparation of these baths, a state of presence and intention is awakened that further enhances their effects. Each ingredient handled with attention and each thought directed during the ritual create a deep harmony with natural forces. This conscious involvement transforms the act of caring for personal energy into a true dialogue with the universe, where desires and intentions are expressed and, consequently, welcomed. Thus, each bath becomes a portal of transformation, allowing cycles to end and new paths of prosperity and well-being to open.

With continuous practice, energy baths cease to be just a purification tool and become a way of life, guided by harmony and respect for the forces of nature. This commitment to self-care and vibrational elevation reinforces the connection with the divine and with one's own essence. By honoring this flow of energy and maintaining clear intention, a fertile inner space is created to cultivate peace, love, health and prosperity. Thus, each drop of consecrated water carries the promise of renewal, guiding the being on a journey of balance and complete fulfillment.

Chapter 21
Color Visualization

Through detailed and in-depth analysis, a clear understanding emerges of how certain events and decisions have shaped the course of history and directly influenced the social, cultural, and economic developments of a society. The interconnection between historical, behavioral, and environmental factors reveals a complex scenario in which each element plays a crucial role in the formation of new ideas, practices, and structures. This panorama demands critical and meticulous reflection on the circumstances that triggered significant changes and on how these transformations impacted the evolution of values and traditions.

By considering the forces that drive transformations over time, it is possible to perceive the importance of understanding not only isolated facts but also the intrinsic relationships between different contexts and protagonists. This approach broadens the perspective on how societies organize, adapt, and overcome challenges, highlighting the constant interaction between past and present. Analyzing the consequences of certain decisions and events provides valuable subsidies for interpreting human behavior and the mechanisms that sustain collective development.

This deep understanding allows us to recognize recurring patterns and identify alternative paths that could have been followed, enriching the perception of the potential for change and innovation. From this comprehensive analysis, a more complete appreciation of social and cultural dynamics develops, providing a solid basis for interpreting events and understanding the complexity inherent in historical processes. Thus, by immersing oneself in this context, space is opened to explore more clearly the motivations, challenges, and results that have shaped the trajectory of societies over time.

Imagine a rainbow appearing before you, its vibrant and luminous colors filling the sky and radiating a soft and comforting energy. Each hue carries a unique frequency, a vibration capable of positively influencing body, mind, and spirit. By visualizing these colors with intention and purpose, you direct these specific vibrations to the energy centers of your body, activating the life force and opening paths for abundance to manifest in your life naturally and fluidly.

Everything in the universe is energy in constant motion, and colors are visible manifestations of this energy vibrating at different frequencies. When you connect with a color through visualization, you are tuning your personal vibration to the frequency of that color. This alignment harmonizes your chakras, dissolves energy blocks, and creates a conducive field to attract what you want to manifest. Thus, color visualization becomes a powerful tool for transformation, capable of balancing emotions, strengthening self-confidence, and enhancing the achievement of goals.

Green, for example, is closely linked to the heart chakra and symbolizes renewal, balance, and growth. By visualizing a soft green light surrounding your body, you connect with the energy of healing and prosperity. This vibration stimulates emotional harmony, strengthens interpersonal relationships, and creates a fertile vibrational field for the flourishing of new financial opportunities. Feel this light filling every cell, dissolving tensions, and opening space for abundance to settle in with lightness and naturalness.

Gold, in turn, represents wealth, personal power, and vitality, being connected to the solar plexus chakra. Imagine yourself bathed in radiant golden light, similar to the sun's rays warming your skin. This energy strengthens your self-confidence, awakens your leadership, and intensifies your capacity for achievement. Visualizing gold around you activates the determination and focus needed to achieve goals and align with the frequency of prosperity and success.

Yellow, also associated with the solar plexus, radiates joy, mental clarity, and creativity. By visualizing an intense yellow glow filling your body, you stimulate the mind to seek creative solutions and maintain optimism in the face of challenges. This luminous vibration unlocks creative flow and attracts new ideas and opportunities, making the internal environment more conducive to personal and professional growth.

Orange, related to the sacral chakra, brings vitality, enthusiasm, and creative impulse. Visualize a warm and vibrant orange light surrounding your abdominal region, activating your creative energy and increasing your disposition. This vibration strengthens self-confidence and expands the ability to transform dreams into concrete actions, favoring the realization of projects and the manifestation of abundance.

Pink, associated with the heart chakra, emanates love, compassion, and harmony. Imagine yourself enveloped in a soft pink mist, like a warm hug. This vibration awakens self-love and heals emotional wounds, opening the heart to healthy and balanced emotional relationships. The energy of pink promotes forgiveness and attracts genuine connections based on respect, affection, and reciprocity.

To fully harness the power of color visualization, it is essential to create a conducive environment. Choose a quiet place where you can relax without interruption. A silent room, an outdoor corner, or even a space decorated with elements that convey calm are ideal. Adjust the lighting to be soft and, if desired, use scents or soft music to enhance the welcoming atmosphere.

Start by focusing on your breathing. Inhale deeply through your nose, feeling the air fill your lungs, and exhale slowly through your mouth, releasing tension. Repeat this process for a few minutes until you feel your mind and body relaxed. This state of calm is essential to deepen the connection with colors.

Intuitively choose the color that best represents what you want to attract or transform. Trust your intuition, as it will guide you to the color most aligned with your needs. With your eyes closed, visualize the chosen color appearing around you, slowly expanding, like a luminous mist or radiant light. Let this color envelop your entire body and penetrate each cell, feeling it dissolve blockages and revitalize your energy.

Feel the vibration of this color. Notice if it brings warmth, coolness, lightness, or vigor. Observe how this energy flows through your body, awakening sensations and dissolving resistance. Direct this color to the chakra corresponding to your goal, visualizing this energy center spinning harmoniously and radiating balance and vitality. If you prefer, conduct the color through all the chakras, feeling each one being nourished and harmonized.

While engaging in this energy, mentally repeat positive affirmations aligned with what you want to manifest. For example, when visualizing the color green, say to yourself: "I am prosperous and open to the opportunities that the universe offers me." Let these words resonate with the vibration of the color, strengthening your intention.

Regular practice of color visualization enhances its effects. Incorporate this technique into your daily or weekly routine, allowing the connection with the energy of colors to deepen and generate positive transformations over time. With discipline and surrender, subtle but powerful changes will begin to manifest in your well-being, emotional balance, and ability to attract abundance.

Setting a clear intention before starting the practice is fundamental. Reflect deeply on your desires and goals. Define your intention positively and directly, creating a focused focus for visualization. This clarity amplifies the power of the practice and directs the energy of color towards the fulfillment of your purpose.

During visualization, maintain your full attention. If scattered thoughts arise, gently return your focus to the color and your intention. Imagine the color with a wealth of detail: feel its texture, temperature, and intensity. The more vivid this image is, the more potent the integration of the color's energy with your vibrational field will be.

Enhance visualization by combining it with other techniques such as mantras, affirmations, or guided meditations. This integration amplifies the impact of the practice, creating an even stronger energy field. Trust your intuition to adapt the practice to your needs.

By delving into this technique, color visualization reveals itself to be more than a mental exercise - it is a channel for inner transformation. Conscious connection with the vibrations of colors allows access to subtle levels of energy, promoting balance between body, mind, and spirit. This alignment favors the manifestation of desires, strengthens self-confidence, and creates a solid foundation for the flourishing of abundance.

With constant practice, you will notice an expansion of consciousness and a deeper relationship with your own essence. Color visualization becomes a tool for self-knowledge, revealing emotional blocks and limiting patterns that can be gently transformed. Each color, with its unique frequency, acts as a bridge between the physical and the emotional, integrating thoughts and feelings in harmony with your goals.

Thus, color visualization not only promotes emotional balance but also expands the ability to create a reality aligned with your most genuine desires. Each breath, each mental image transforms into a seed of transformation, allowing balance and prosperity to flourish authentically and lastingly.

By delving into the practice of color visualization, it becomes evident that this exercise is not limited to aesthetic contemplation but acts as a powerful channel for inner transformation. The conscious connection with the vibrations of colors allows access to more subtle levels of energy, favoring the alignment between mind, body, and spirit. This process not only enhances the manifestation of desires but also promotes a state of balance that reverberates positively in all areas of life. Each color, with its unique frequency, acts as a bridge between the physical and emotional world, facilitating the integration of feelings, thoughts, and actions in harmony with personal goals.

With continued practice, color visualization proves to be an essential tool for self-knowledge and the expansion of consciousness. By perceiving the responses of the body and mind during these visualizations, it is possible to identify emotional blocks, limiting beliefs, and behavior patterns that can be gently transformed. This gradual awakening promotes a deeper relationship with one's own essence and broadens the perception of how external and internal energies influence the flow of life. Thus, cultivating this conscious connection not only strengthens emotional balance but also expands the ability to create a reality aligned with one's most genuine desires.

This path of energy integration unfolds as a continuous journey of healing and growth. By incorporating color visualization as part of a self-care routine, space is opened for energy to flow freely, nourishing every aspect of being. Constant practice reinforces the perception that abundance, harmony, and well-being are natural states that can be cultivated with intention and presence. Thus, each breath and each mental image become seeds of transformation, allowing balance and prosperity to flourish authentically and lastingly.

Chapter 22
Continuous Learning

Continuous learning represents a daily commitment to personal and professional growth, essential to thrive in a dynamic and competitive world. Developing this mindset means integrating knowledge as a fundamental part of life, constantly seeking new skills, staying updated on trends, and improving skills that drive success. This active stance towards learning allows you to explore diverse opportunities, adapt to changes, and build a solid path towards full achievement. By investing time and energy in continuous development, each achievement becomes a direct reflection of this effort, broadening horizons and opening doors to a more prosperous and fulfilling future.

Adopting continuous learning as a constant practice strengthens the capacity for innovation, resilience, and adaptability. This process broadens the worldview, stimulates creativity, and allows for finding strategic solutions to complex challenges. Mastering new tools, methodologies, and knowledge puts the individual at a competitive advantage, making them more prepared to deal with technological transformations and market demands. More than accumulating information, continuous learning drives the practical application of knowledge, favoring concrete and impactful results in various areas of life.

In addition to enhancing your career, continuous learning promotes self-confidence and personal satisfaction. Constant evolution strengthens self-esteem and awakens a proactive stance towards challenges, stimulating the pursuit of more ambitious goals. This journey of growth provides a balance between professional development and personal fulfillment, creating a positive cycle of motivation and achievement. By turning learning into a daily habit, it is possible to build a solid path to success, with more purpose, autonomy, and fulfillment.

Imagine a vast garden where each plant flourishes according to the care it receives. Just as a dedicated gardener waters, prunes, fertilizes, and protects their plants from pests, the human mind also needs constant stimulation to grow and flourish. Continuous learning functions as the essential nutrient that feeds the intellect, providing personal and professional growth. By investing in the acquisition of new knowledge and skills, a solid foundation is created to explore opportunities and reach maximum potential. Each new piece of information assimilated acts like a drop of water or a ray of sunshine, strengthening the roots of knowledge and driving the flourishing of ideas and achievements. This constant care with one's own evolution not only broadens horizons but also opens paths to a more abundant and fulfilling life.

In the context of an increasingly dynamic and competitive labor market, continuous learning becomes an indispensable tool for those who want to stand out and achieve success. Investing in self-development is like fertilizing the soil of a garden: it strengthens the base and prepares the ground for more generous harvests. Professionals who constantly seek new knowledge significantly increase their employability, becoming more competitive and valued. The constant updating of skills enables them to occupy strategic positions, explore innovative sectors, and negotiate more advantageous working conditions. This proactive stance is perceived by companies as a differential, highlighting these individuals as strategic resources with high growth potential.

In addition to opening doors in the job market, continuous learning refines professional performance. The constant search for improvement allows for the mastery of advanced techniques, familiarity with modern tools, and the adoption of more efficient methods. This process results in greater productivity, quality in deliveries, and agility in problem-solving. Just as a gardener who learns to identify the right time for pruning to stimulate the healthy growth of plants, the professional who improves their skills knows how to optimize processes and avoid mistakes, delivering superior results and consolidating their position within the organization.

Exposure to new knowledge also functions as a creative pruning, allowing ideas to flourish in unexpected ways. By exploring different cultures, concepts, and experiences, the mind expands and connects information in innovative ways. This fertile environment fuels creativity, facilitating the creation of original and adaptable solutions to complex problems. As in a diverse garden, where different species coexist and enrich the ecosystem, the diversity of knowledge acquired through continuous learning stimulates experimentation and critical thinking, essential for innovation in products, services, and processes.

Constant development also cultivates self-confidence. By mastering new skills and understanding new concepts, the individual strengthens their self-esteem and begins to face challenges with more confidence. This confidence is reflected in a proactive stance, a willingness to take on greater responsibilities, and resilience in the face of obstacles. Just as a robust plant resists strong winds because it has deep roots, the self-confident professional stands firm in the face of adversity and is more receptive to growth opportunities. The feeling of continuous progress reinforces belief in one's own abilities and fuels the desire to move forward.

Adaptability, in turn, is a direct reflection of this growth process. In a constantly changing world, the ability to quickly adjust to new realities is vital. Continuous learning functions as an adaptation tool, allowing professionals to incorporate innovations, keep up with technological changes, and understand new market dynamics. This flexibility guarantees not only survival in a challenging environment but also leadership in change processes. Just as a plant leans towards the light to continue growing, the adaptable professional adjusts their trajectory according to the demands of the environment, remaining relevant and competitive.

By expanding their skills, the individual also expands their field of activity. The development of new skills works like planting different seeds in the same garden, resulting in multiple possibilities for flowering. This plurality of knowledge opens doors to explore different areas, sectors, and functions, allowing for professional rediscoveries and even entrepreneurship. Thus, new paths are revealed, aligning with personal interests and values, and creating opportunities for fulfillment that previously seemed distant.

To cultivate this continuous cycle of learning, it is essential to define clear objectives. Just as the gardener plans the cultivation of each plant, establishing what they want to harvest, the individual needs to identify their goals and understand what knowledge and skills are needed to achieve them. Defining specific and measurable objectives directs efforts and keeps motivation alive throughout the development journey. This planning functions as a map that guides the way, allowing for constant and safe progress.

With well-defined goals, it becomes essential to draw up a detailed development plan. Dividing large objectives into smaller steps and setting realistic deadlines creates a constant rhythm of evolution. Including varied resources such as courses, books, events, and mentoring enriches the process and provides diversified learning. This strategic planning works like a gardener's calendar, which organizes the care of each plant according to the seasons, ensuring that all receive the necessary attention to grow.

Exploring different learning methods keeps the process dynamic and engaging. Just as a garden thrives with the combination of sunlight, water, and nutrients, the mind is strengthened by being stimulated by multiple sources of knowledge. Participating in online courses, face-to-face workshops, specialized readings, podcasts, and educational videos broadens understanding of topics and avoids monotony. The variety of methods also allows you to discover new ways of learning, making the journey richer and more effective.

Applying the acquired knowledge is like reaping the fruits of careful cultivation. True assimilation of learning occurs when knowledge is put into practice. Whether in personal projects, in the professional environment, or in volunteer activities, this application strengthens understanding and allows for adjustments to improve skills. This cycle of learning and practice consolidates knowledge and promotes continuous growth.

Sharing what you learn is also part of this process. By sharing knowledge with others, whether in conversations, debates, or mentoring, understanding is reinforced, and critical thinking is stimulated. This exchange of ideas not only solidifies learning but also contributes to collective development. Just as plants share nutrients through interconnected roots, the sharing of knowledge creates a network of mutual growth.

Finally, celebrating achievements along the learning journey is essential. Each new piece of knowledge assimilated, each skill developed represents a victory that deserves to be recognized. Celebrating this progress keeps motivation high and reinforces commitment to continuous development. Just as the gardener appreciates each flower that blooms, valuing each advance fuels the enthusiasm to continue cultivating one's own growth.

Integrating continuous learning into everyday life requires discipline and commitment, but the fruits harvested along this journey are valuable and transformative. Small daily advances accumulate and generate profound impacts on how we deal with challenges and take advantage of opportunities. This constant cycle of evolution expands our ability to see beyond the obvious, favoring more assertive and strategic choices. In this way, the acquired knowledge not only adds value to the professional trajectory but also shapes a more resilient mindset open to new possibilities.

Throughout this process, it is important to recognize that learning does not occur linearly. There will be moments of doubt, adjustments, and even setbacks, but each experience contributes to strengthening skills and self-knowledge. Facing these challenges with flexibility and curiosity transforms obstacles into valuable lessons. Thus, the search for growth becomes a continuous path of self-discovery, in which each stage overcome reaffirms the importance of moving forward with determination and enthusiasm.

In this scenario, continuous learning ceases to be just a tool for professional development and becomes a way of life. It fuels the desire to grow, inspires positive changes, and strengthens confidence to tread new paths. By cultivating this mindset, we open doors to enriching experiences and build a legacy of constant evolution, capable of impacting not only our own trajectory but also the environment around us.

Chapter 23
Giving and Sharing

The practice of giving and sharing profoundly strengthens the flow of abundance in life, creating authentic connections and promoting collective well-being. By offering time, resources, or talents, a continuous cycle of prosperity is established, where each gesture of generosity not only benefits the receiver but also expands the giver's potential. This movement of sincere giving transforms simple actions into powerful instruments of change, reflecting a genuine commitment to building a more just, supportive, and balanced society. Generosity manifests as an essential link that connects individuals to enriching opportunities and experiences, promoting personal and collective growth.

When attitudes of giving are incorporated into everyday life, they become part of a natural process of valuing what one already has and opening up to new achievements. This willingness to contribute activates a positive flow, which attracts new possibilities and strengthens the feeling of fulfillment and purpose. Each act of sharing not only meets immediate needs but also inspires others to adopt similar behaviors, creating a continuous chain of support and collaboration. Thus, generosity multiplies, positively impacting entire communities and reinforcing interpersonal bonds based on respect and empathy.

In addition to directly benefiting the recipient, the practice of giving and sharing provides emotional and spiritual growth for those who practice these gestures. By dedicating time and resources to the collective good, one develops a more sensitive outlook to the needs of others and a deeper understanding of the individual role in building a more harmonious world. This process awakens awareness of the importance of community, promotes emotional balance, and strengthens fundamental values such as compassion, gratitude, and social responsibility. Thus, giving and sharing are consolidated as powerful paths to achieving a full life, filled with meaning and abundance.

Imagine a mighty river that follows its course, flowing into the sea and carrying with it nutrients that feed the life around it. This river does not deplete itself by sharing its waters; on the contrary, its flow is renewed and strengthened, perpetuating the cycle of abundance. So too is the practice of giving and sharing: by generously offering part of our resources, time, or talents, we nourish other lives and, simultaneously, strengthen our own flow of prosperity. Each gesture of generosity reverberates like gentle waves, reaching distant places and promoting profound transformations, not only in those who receive but also in those who give.

Acts of generosity have the power to raise our vibration and align our thoughts and emotions with the frequency of prosperity. When we give something with an open heart, expecting nothing in return, we create an inner harmony that attracts positive opportunities and reinforces confidence in our own worth. It is as if, by planting a seed of kindness, we are cultivating a fertile field of possibilities that naturally flourish in our lives. This alignment with abundance makes us more receptive to the new and more confident to follow paths that previously seemed distant.

Furthermore, giving and sharing are sincere expressions of gratitude. By acknowledging the achievements that are already part of our lives, we open space for new blessings to arrive. This recognition transforms the perception of what we have: what previously seemed sufficient becomes seen as abundant. Gratitude creates an environment conducive to growth, as it teaches us to value the present and to trust that there is always more to be achieved. Just as the river does not keep its waters but delivers them to the ocean, so too should we allow generosity to flow freely, renewing the cycle of abundance.

Generosity also has the power to create and strengthen genuine connections. By sharing resources, time, or knowledge, we build solid bridges based on empathy and mutual respect. These sincere relationships form a support network that can open doors to new personal and professional opportunities. Like underground roots that intertwine and support large trees, human connections, nurtured by generous gestures, strengthen the sense of belonging and stimulate collaboration in our communities.

The impact of sharing prosperity goes beyond the immediate circle of those who receive. Our gestures inspire others to do the same, creating a chain of solidarity that continually expands. By demonstrating that abundance is accessible to all, we motivate others to adopt generous attitudes. Thus, the impact of a single action multiplies, reverberating in different directions and generating collective benefits. This movement of inspiration transforms small gestures into great social changes, reinforcing the idea that each contribution, however small, has immeasurable value.

Giving and sharing are also powerful instruments for strengthening communities. When we invest our time, resources, or skills in social causes, we contribute to creating a more just and balanced environment. Strengthening communities promotes equal opportunities and improves the quality of life for all its members. As in a well-cared-for ecosystem, where each living being plays a fundamental role, a supportive society grows in a healthy and resilient way, allowing everyone to prosper together.

In addition to the social impact, scientific studies prove that acts of generosity increase our happiness. The practice of giving activates areas of the brain associated with pleasure and well-being, releasing endorphins that provide a lasting feeling of joy. This happiness is not limited to fleeting moments but contributes to a more balanced mental health and a more fulfilling life. Just as the river feels lightness as it follows its course, we too experience lightness and fullness when sharing with others.

There are several ways to practice generosity. Financial donation is one of them, allowing support for social causes, community projects, and charities. Small regular contributions can generate major transformations when carried out with purpose and consistency. Just as a drop of water contributes to filling a river, each donated amount, however small, adds to a collective effort capable of changing lives.

Volunteering is another powerful expression of generosity. Dedicating time and skills to help in social projects, community events, or non-profit organizations allows one to experience different realities, develop empathy, and create meaningful connections. By donating our time, we not only help others but also enrich our own journey with transformative experiences.

The donation of material goods also has a relevant impact. Clothes, food, books, or objects that we no longer use can gain new meaning when destined for those in need. This simple gesture avoids waste and meets basic needs, in addition to encouraging conscious consumption and social responsibility.

Sharing knowledge is another way to promote collective well-being. Sharing knowledge through mentoring, workshops, or lectures expands learning and empowers others to achieve their goals. By teaching, we reinforce our own understanding and contribute to building a more educated and collaborative society.

Simple gestures of kindness in everyday life also have transformative power. Helping someone with groceries, giving up your seat on public transport, or offering a smile are attitudes that create a more supportive and welcoming environment. These small actions inspire others to do good, creating a support network based on empathy.

Taking time to listen and emotionally support those in need is a valuable way to share. Being there for a friend, visiting someone who feels lonely, or simply offering company are gestures that strengthen emotional bonds and combat social isolation. This type of care demonstrates genuine attention and reinforces the importance of human connections.

Sharing material resources, such as tools, books, or spaces, promotes collectiveness and encourages the conscious use of goods. By sharing what we have, we contribute to creating a culture of cooperation and sustainability, where everyone can benefit in a fair and balanced way.

For generosity to be a constant part of life, it is important to give from the heart. Practicing giving in a sincere and spontaneous way enhances the positive impact and strengthens our connection to abundance. Choosing causes that resonate with our values makes the act of giving even more meaningful, as it involves us in a deep and authentic way.

Exploring creative ways to give expands our reach. Organizing campaigns, promoting fundraising, or using social media to mobilize help are innovative ways to inspire others to participate. Starting with small gestures and maintaining consistency reinforces the commitment to the collective good, while sharing our experiences inspires more people to follow the same path.

By integrating the practice of giving and sharing into our routine, we understand that true abundance is not in accumulation but in the ability to distribute and support mutual growth. Each gesture of generosity is transformed into a planted seed, capable of flourishing into new opportunities and strengthening the hope for a more just and supportive future. Thus, we cultivate a world where prosperity is shared and where true success is measured by the positive impact we leave on the lives around us.

By integrating giving and sharing into your life, you realize that these acts transcend the simple material gesture, becoming part of a greater purpose. Each contribution, however small it may seem, reverberates positively, creating a cycle of benefits that reaches individuals, communities, and, consequently, the world. True abundance lies not only in the accumulation of goods, but in the ability to distribute, support, and encourage mutual growth. This understanding broadens the vision of prosperity, transforming it into something collective, accessible, and sustainable.

The constant practice of generosity also awakens a sense of responsibility for collective well-being, reinforcing the idea that everyone has a fundamental role to play in building a more egalitarian society. When the act of giving becomes part of the routine, it creates deep roots that strengthen not only those who receive, but also those who offer. This natural balance between giving and receiving nourishes an environment where empathy flourishes and solidarity expands, forming solid foundations for a more harmonious and respectful coexistence.

Thus, by choosing to give and share authentically, a path of personal and collective growth is opened, where each gesture contributes to a more humane and prosperous world. True abundance manifests itself when we understand that to prosper is to walk together, nurturing networks of support, trust, and inspiration. On this journey, each generous action is transformed into a seed of change, capable of flourishing into new possibilities and strengthening the hope for a more just and supportive future.

Chapter 24
Creating Opportunities

Abundance is a direct result of intentional actions and the commitment to transforming ideas into reality. By adopting a proactive and determined stance, it is possible to open paths to growth and new achievements in various areas of life. This process requires initiative, creativity, and the willingness to take calculated risks, allowing each step taken to become a concrete opportunity for evolution. When acting with clarity of purpose and dedication, the surrounding environment responds, creating favorable conditions for success and prosperity to manifest consistently. Thus, the construction of opportunities becomes a continuous practice, where each strategic decision expands the possibilities of personal and professional fulfillment.

Creating opportunities involves more than waiting for circumstances to change; it is about acting with focus and planning to generate effective changes. This requires identifying talents, strengthening skills, and exploring innovative ways that can connect dreams to concrete results. The constant search for knowledge and the cultivation of solid relationships are essential tools in this process, as they broaden perspectives and facilitate access to new possibilities. Each action taken with courage and intention not only brings you closer to your desired goals but also strengthens self-confidence and resilience in the face of challenges, transforming obstacles into impulses for growth.

By maintaining an open and adaptable mindset, it becomes possible to see opportunities even in the most challenging situations. Success arises from the sum of small daily actions carried out with persistence and enthusiasm, creating a continuous cycle of evolution. The boldness to propose solutions, experiment with new ideas, and act ethically builds a solid foundation for achieving ambitious goals. Thus, the path to abundance is paved by consistent attitudes and the ability to transform each experience into learning and progress, making the creation of opportunities a natural and constant process.

Imagine a farmer who, even before throwing his seeds into the ground, dedicates time to preparing the land with care. He plows the soil, removes impurities, chooses the best seeds, and patiently irrigates the plantation, attentive to changes in the weather and the needs of the plants. This farmer does not depend on chance to harvest good fruits; he creates the ideal conditions for an abundant harvest. So too is the process of creating opportunities in life: it requires preparation, dedication, and constant action. It is not enough to wait for circumstances to change. It is necessary to act with purpose, sow ideas, nurture projects, and take care of each stage until the results flourish.

Taking responsibility for creating opportunities means leaving the spectator position and becoming the protagonist of your own story. It is about acting with intention, identifying and cultivating possibilities that can transform dreams into reality. When you decide to leave your comfort zone and explore new paths, you significantly broaden your horizon of possibilities. This movement allows you to discover hidden talents, acquire unknown skills, and get involved in innovative projects that previously seemed distant. Just as a new seed can surprise with never-before-seen flowers, each experience lived with courage and curiosity opens doors to previously unimaginable achievements.

Seeking new opportunities also fuels creativity. When faced with challenges and seeking solutions, the mind is encouraged to think differently, connecting ideas from different fields and adapting old concepts to new realities. Creativity, in this context, is like the fertile ground that welcomes the seed: the more well-cared for and diversified, the richer the harvest will be. Allowing yourself to experiment, take risks, and learn from each attempt strengthens this ability, making it essential to transform obstacles into concrete possibilities.

Each step taken towards your goals strengthens your self-confidence. By achieving small goals, you validate your ability to make significant changes in your life. This inner strengthening translates into the way you face challenges: with more courage, willingness to take risks, and faith in your potential. Just as the farmer observes the first shoots and feels certain that the harvest will come, each small victory reinforces the belief that great achievements are possible.

Demonstrating initiative and determination is sending a clear signal to the universe that you are ready to receive and take advantage of new opportunities. This alignment of action and purpose creates a positive flow, attracting connections, resources, and favorable situations. It is like a well-cultivated field that attracts rain at the right time: the more you act with focus, the more doors open, allowing abundance to flow naturally in all areas of your life.

For this cycle of creating opportunities to happen consistently, it is essential to start with clear objectives. Setting concrete and specific goals works like the farmer who carefully chooses which seeds to plant. Knowing exactly where you want to go directs your efforts and makes the path to your goals more effective. With well-defined deadlines and steps, your actions gain focus and become more strategic.

Identifying your passions and talents is also an essential step. When you recognize what truly excites you and the skills you excel at, it becomes possible to align these elements with projects that have meaning. This balance between passion and competence keeps motivation high and creates a solid foundation for achieving success. Just as the farmer chooses crops suitable for the climate and soil, directing efforts to areas where you have affinity increases the chances of consistent growth.

Expanding your network of contacts is another vital practice. Building relationships with people who share similar interests or who can open doors to new opportunities strengthens your path. Participating in events, joining communities, or simply being open to dialogue expands connections and enhances the chances of personal and professional development. Just as the farmer connects with other producers to learn new techniques, networking allows the exchange of experiences and access to valuable resources.

Continuous learning is the fertilizer in this process. Investing in courses, readings, and experiences expands your skills and keeps you up-to-date with market trends. Being prepared with new knowledge increases your competitiveness and opens space for innovative solutions. The more you dedicate yourself to learning, the more fertile the soil becomes where your ideas can grow.

Proactivity is the water that makes the seed germinate. Not waiting for opportunities to appear, but going to meet them, is what transforms intentions into results. Proposing projects, suggesting improvements, presenting ideas, and actively seeking new possibilities are attitudes that drive progress. Just as the farmer who does not wait for rain but irrigates his field, you need to act for opportunities to flourish.

Being persistent in the face of challenges is another fundamental pillar. Obstacles are inevitable, but persistence is what differentiates those who achieve their goals from those who give up along the way. Each difficulty faced is an opportunity for learning and adjusting strategies. Just as the farmer faces pests and bad weather but adapts his methods to protect the harvest, you must learn from challenges and keep moving forward with focus and resilience.

It is also necessary to take advantage of the opportunities that arise, even if they are not directly aligned with your initial objectives. Often, the best chances appear unexpectedly and can open up even more promising paths. The flexibility to recognize and embrace these moments is crucial. Just as a plant adapts to the soil where it was thrown, being flexible in the face of new circumstances allows you to grow in any terrain.

Courage is the final impulse that transforms planning into action. Facing fears, leaving your comfort zone, and making bold decisions are essential attitudes to create and seize opportunities. Trusting your potential and embracing challenges is like the farmer who decides to plant a new crop, even without guarantees of favorable weather. It is this courage that allows you to explore new possibilities and achieve great results.

Maintaining a positive attitude along the way is equally important. Optimism strengthens resilience and influences how you are perceived by those around you. Believing in your potential creates an environment conducive to new possibilities. Just as the sun illuminates and warms the plantation, positivity nourishes the soil where opportunities can flourish.

Finally, the creation of opportunities is a collaborative process. Being surrounded by people who share similar values enhances the achievement of your goals. Genuine relationships and sincere exchanges create a fertile environment for new ideas and projects. Thus, by combining your personal initiative with the power of collaboration, you strengthen your trajectory and transform challenges into possibilities.

Therefore, creating opportunities is more than an isolated act: it is a lifestyle. Each strategic decision, each risk taken, and each step taken with purpose form the solid path to a life full of achievements. Just as a generous harvest is the result of constant care, abundance manifests itself for those who cultivate, with dedication and courage, the fertile ground of opportunities.

Creating opportunities is a continuous exercise in self-knowledge and directed action. By recognizing your achievements and learning from the challenges you face, you strengthen the foundation to move forward with more confidence and clarity. Each experience lived, whether of success or overcoming, contributes to shaping a resilient and strategic mindset. This cycle of constant learning expands your ability to identify opportune moments and act with confidence, making the journey towards abundance more consistent and meaningful.

Furthermore, it is essential to value small victories along the way, as they are what maintain enthusiasm and fuel motivation to move forward. Each step taken with purpose reinforces the commitment to your goals and creates a cumulative effect of progress. The celebration of these achievements not only strengthens self-confidence but also inspires new ideas and drives the pursuit of even more expressive results. Thus, the path to growth becomes lighter and more rewarding, allowing you to continue moving forward with determination.

Finally, remembering that creating opportunities is a collaborative process can open unimaginable doors. Surrounding yourself with people who share similar values and goals enhances the achievement of goals and stimulates mutual development. Genuine connections and the exchange of experiences create a fertile environment for the emergence of new ideas and projects. Thus, by combining personal initiative with the power of collaboration, you strengthen your trajectory, transform challenges into possibilities, and build, day after day, the solid path to a life full of abundance and achievements.

Chapter 25
Celebrating Success

Recognizing and celebrating your own success is fundamental to consolidating achievements and driving new progress. Each goal achieved represents the result of effort, dedication, and overcoming challenges, making it essential to value these moments as part of the growth process. By celebrating victories, you strengthen self-confidence, reinforce motivation, and create a positive cycle that encourages the pursuit of new goals. This personal recognition not only validates the journey taken but also expands the perception of deservingness, making the path to success lighter and more satisfying.

The celebration of achievements goes beyond a simple act of commemoration; it serves as a powerful tool for continuous encouragement. By valuing your own results, however small, you develop a mindset of abundance that attracts even more opportunities. This habit of gratitude and self-recognition awakens a positive energy that directly influences how future challenges are faced. Celebrating success is a constant reminder that progress is being made and that each step taken brings you closer to your desired dreams.

Allowing yourself to celebrate is also a way to maintain balance between effort and reward, recognizing the importance of rest and pleasure along the way. This practice strengthens not only emotional well-being but also stimulates creativity and willingness to face new challenges. By valuing each stage achieved, you build a solid foundation of self-confidence and enthusiasm, creating an environment conducive to continuing to move forward with determination. In this way, celebrating success becomes an essential act to maintain motivation and open paths to even greater achievements.

Imagine an athlete crossing the finish line after a long and exhausting competition. When raising the trophy, he celebrates not only the momentary victory but the entire path traveled—the daily training sessions, the pain overcome, the defeats that taught him, and the small achievements that propelled him. This moment of celebration is a consecration of effort and a reaffirmation that he is capable of going further. Similarly, celebrating every achievement, no matter how small, is essential to nurture self-confidence, reinforce belief in one's potential, and pave the way for new victories.

Celebrating success is not just an act of commemoration; it is a powerful tool for personal empowerment. Each recognized victory, big or small, validates the effort invested and reinforces the certainty that the path taken is the right one. This recognition creates a mindset of abundance, where each achievement becomes fuel for new goals. Just as the athlete who feels the urge to seek new challenges after savoring victory, you will also feel more motivated to move forward, knowing that you are capable of overcoming obstacles and accomplishing great things.

Recognizing your own merit strengthens self-confidence. By valuing your achievements, you reinforce the perception that you are worthy of achieving what you desire. This internal validation expands your ability to face challenges with courage and determination. Each celebration becomes a confirmation that the effort is worth it, strengthening resilience in the face of adversity. It is as if, with each step conquered, you build a solid foundation upon which new opportunities and challenges can be faced with greater security.

In addition to strengthening self-confidence, celebrating success creates a virtuous cycle of positivity. The energy generated by the recognition of each achievement multiplies, attracting even more prosperity and opportunities. This constant flow of gratitude and enthusiasm broadens your perception of what is possible to achieve, making the process of reaching goals lighter and more enjoyable. The more you celebrate, the more motivated you feel to keep moving forward, nurturing a continuous cycle of growth.

Sharing victories with others further enhances this process. Sharing moments of success with family, friends, and colleagues creates deeper connections and inspires those around you. When you celebrate together, you build an environment of mutual support and collective motivation, where each individual achievement contributes to the growth of all. Just like a crowd that vibrates with the athlete's victory, the support of the people around you strengthens confidence and encourages the pursuit of new challenges.

To celebrate success meaningfully, it is important to recognize every achievement, regardless of size. Valuing every step forward, every obstacle overcome, and every lesson learned is essential to maintain enthusiasm and motivation. This constant recognition reinforces commitment to your goals and transforms progress into something tangible, capable of driving new steps.

Expressing gratitude is another fundamental aspect of celebration. Thanking yourself for the dedicated effort, the people who supported your journey, and the opportunities that arose expands the feeling of accomplishment. Gratitude creates a positive flow of energy, opening space for new achievements and strengthening the abundance mindset. This genuine feeling of appreciation transforms the journey traveled into a constant source of inspiration.

Rewarding yourself for each goal achieved is a concrete way to recognize your commitment. Choosing a meaningful reward, whether it's a special experience, a moment of self-care, or the fulfillment of a long-held wish, reinforces the value of achievement. This gesture of self-recognition functions as a positive stimulus, encouraging discipline and motivation to face new challenges. Thus, you remember that each victory deserves to be celebrated in a unique way.

Recording your achievements is also an effective way to keep motivation alive. Documenting your victories in a journal, mural, or album creates a visual and emotional space where you can revisit your progress whenever you need inspiration. This record serves as concrete proof of how much you have evolved, reinforcing self-confidence and renewing commitment to your future goals.

Creating celebration rituals makes each victory even more meaningful. Whether it's lighting a candle, making a toast, listening to special music, or engaging in a pleasurable activity, these rituals symbolize your achievements and create emotional memories. Incorporating practices that represent your success strengthens the emotional significance of victories and transforms the act of celebrating into a unique and remarkable experience.

Allowing yourself moments of rest and fun after achieving an important goal is also essential. The balance between effort and reward is crucial for maintaining physical and emotional well-being. Setting aside time to relax and enjoy leisure time renews energy and prevents burnout, preparing you to face new challenges with more willingness.

After each celebration, it is important to review your goals. Reflecting on the journey traveled and adjusting the next steps allows you to identify new opportunities for growth. This continuous process of evaluation and planning ensures that you stay aligned with your dreams and challenges, keeping the cycle of progress in constant motion.

Celebrating small progress along the way is as important as celebrating big achievements. Every step forward, no matter how small, represents an essential step towards your goals. Valuing these moments keeps motivation high and reinforces the importance of consistency. Thus, you recognize that every small victory contributes to building great results.

Similarly, celebrating overcome challenges is fundamental. Each obstacle overcome proves your strength and ability to adapt. By recognizing these overcomings, you transform difficulties into valuable lessons, strengthening your self-confidence and preparing you to face new challenges with more courage.

More than celebrating results, it is essential to value the journey. True fulfillment lies in appreciating each step of the way, with its lessons and experiences. Celebrating the process makes the journey lighter and more enjoyable, reducing anxiety about the future and allowing you to fully experience each moment.

Incorporating celebration into everyday life transforms success into a continuous and pleasurable process. This habit allows you to recognize the value of daily effort, transforming the path into something as rewarding as the arrival. Celebrating thus becomes a bridge between what has already been achieved and what is yet to come, nurturing motivation and renewing enthusiasm to keep moving forward.

By understanding that each victory carries important lessons, you strengthen a mindset of constant growth. Celebrating is not just about celebrating results, but honoring the process, the choices, and the adjustments made along the way. This balance between effort and recognition sustains lasting achievements and drives the pursuit of more ambitious challenges.

Allowing yourself to celebrate is, above all, respecting your own history. It is recognizing how much you have evolved and valuing every step taken. It is in this space of gratitude and recognition that new ideas are born, energies are renewed, and confidence to move forward is strengthened. Each celebration is a powerful reminder that you are capable of going further, consolidating the path to a life full of meaning, prosperity, and accomplishments.

By incorporating celebration as a natural part of the journey, you begin to see success not as a final destination, but as a continuous construction. This attentive look at each achievement allows you to recognize the value of daily effort and transforms the path into something as rewarding as the arrival itself. Thus, celebration becomes a bridge between what has already been achieved and what is yet to come, nurturing motivation and renewing enthusiasm to face new challenges with confidence and determination.

Furthermore, understanding that each victory carries essential lessons strengthens the mindset of constant evolution. Celebrating is not just about recognizing results, but also honoring the process, the choices, and the adaptations made along the way. This balance between effort and recognition creates a solid foundation to sustain lasting achievements and drives the pursuit of more challenging goals, with the certainty that each step, however small, contributes to building a successful journey.

Therefore, allowing yourself to celebrate is respecting your own history and recognizing how much you have evolved. It is in this space of gratitude and self-worth that new ideas arise, energies are renewed, and confidence to move forward is strengthened. Thus, each celebration becomes a powerful reminder that you are capable of achieving even more, consolidating the path to a life full of meaning, prosperity, and genuine achievements.

Chapter 26
Attitude of Gratitude

Gratitude is a transformative force that enhances the way life unfolds, creating a constant flow of abundance and well-being. Recognizing and valuing every achievement, every act of kindness, and every opportunity received strengthens a deep connection with all that has already been achieved. This awareness activates a positive cycle in which sincere appreciation for small and large blessings naturally attracts new enriching experiences. Just as fertile ground welcomes seeds that grow and flourish, the grateful mind becomes fertile ground for prosperity, joy, and continuous achievements.

By adopting gratitude as a way of life, it is possible to realize that every aspect of life—from challenging situations to the simplest moments—carries valuable lessons and opportunities for growth. This perspective broadens the vision of one's own path, allowing obstacles to be seen as stepping stones for personal development. With this understanding, the incessant search for more transforms into contentment with what one already has, generating balance and harmony. This state of genuine appreciation creates space for new opportunities to emerge naturally and fluidly.

Living with gratitude means aligning thoughts and emotions with a positive vibration that reverberates in all areas of life. This alignment strengthens emotional, physical, and spiritual health, providing mental clarity, serenity, and willingness to face daily challenges. By nurturing this feeling, each achievement becomes more meaningful and each interaction deeper. Thus, gratitude becomes not just a response to positive events, but a daily and conscious choice to recognize the value present in every moment of the journey.

Imagine a glass, clear and full to the brim with crystal clear water. When trying to add more water, it will inevitably overflow, running down the sides and being lost. The same happens with life when you do not recognize and value the abundance already present. Ignoring the blessings that surround everyday life is like trying to fill this glass without realizing that it is already full. Gratitude acts as the gesture of stopping, observing, and appreciating the fullness of this glass, creating space for new experiences to be welcomed. By sincerely acknowledging what you already have, you pave the way for the universe to continue to offer more blessings, allowing the manifestation of dreams and the construction of the desired life.

This attitude of gratitude goes far beyond a momentary feeling; it represents a conscious decision to direct focus to what is positive and abundant. It is like opening a window and allowing sunlight to illuminate the interior of a previously dark room. By cultivating this attentive look at small and large blessings, personal vibration rises, creating an energy field that naturally attracts new opportunities. This heightened state of awareness not only broadens perception of the world around you, but also attunes mind and body to possibilities that previously seemed distant. Life then flows more lightly, and goals become more accessible, like ripe fruits ready to be picked.

In addition to influencing the emotional sphere, gratitude has profound effects on physical health. Practicing it regularly triggers positive reactions in the body, reducing the production of stress-related hormones, such as cortisol, and stimulating the release of beneficial substances, such as serotonin and dopamine. This chemical balance strengthens the immune system, increasing the production of antibodies and defense cells. Thus, gratitude becomes a silent ally in the prevention of diseases and the promotion of more robust health, creating an invisible armor that protects the body and mind.

Serenity also finds fertile ground in the constant practice of gratitude. By shifting focus away from excessive worries and negative thoughts, the mind begins to inhabit the present more and anxiety scenarios less. This mental redirection softens the weight of everyday life, allowing challenges to be faced with more calmness and clarity. Like a gentle breeze that dispels the fog, gratitude clears the path, making it less arduous and more understandable.

The reflection of this serenity extends to nighttime rest. Incorporating gratitude into your routine before bed transforms rest time into a restorative pause. By mentally revisiting the positive events of the day, the mind calms down, dissolving anxieties and promoting deep and restful sleep. This simple practice is like cradling one's soul in comfort, ensuring that dawn brings more willingness and encouragement to face the new day.

Recognizing your own achievements, however small, significantly strengthens self-esteem. With each valued step, self-confidence expands, shaping a more secure posture towards life. Celebrating daily victories, even discreet ones, is like planting seeds that, over time, grow and transform into a forest of self-love and determination. This process nourishes the perception of personal value and expands the ability to face challenges with firmness and courage.

In relationships, gratitude presents itself as an invisible link that strengthens emotional bonds. Small gestures of recognition, such as a sincere thank you or a spontaneous compliment, create bridges of empathy and reciprocity. These gestures, however simple, have the power to soften conflicts, deepen connections, and transform the surrounding environment into a more harmonious and welcoming space. Shared gratitude multiplies, reverberating in more authentic and sustainable relationships.

At the same time, this continuous practice of recognizing and valuing what you have awakens genuine happiness. Gratitude expands the ability to find joy in small things, transforming everyday life into a scenario full of precious moments. The optimistic perception that arises from this constant appreciation reshapes the way you see life, cultivating lasting contentment that does not depend on external circumstances.

To nurture this state of gratitude, small daily habits make all the difference. Keeping a gratitude journal, for example, is a practical way to record the experiences, people, and moments that awaken this feeling. Writing about the simplicity of a hot coffee in the morning or about a pleasant conversation with a friend reinforces the perception that there is always something to be thankful for. This daily reflection exercise strengthens the mind to perceive new reasons to feel grateful, creating a virtuous cycle of appreciation.

Another effective practice is to give thanks before bed. By closing your eyes and mentally revisiting the small victories and lessons learned throughout the day, the mind calms down and the body prepares for a deeper rest. This moment of reflection not only improves the quality of sleep, but also prepares the subconscious to awaken with more lightness and willingness.

Expressing gratitude to others is also essential. Not letting recognition remain only in thought, but verbalizing it, makes the feeling even more powerful. A simple "thank you" or a sincere compliment can strengthen bonds and spread positivity around. This gesture, when genuine, creates a cycle of good energies, nurturing relationships and making environments lighter.

Writing gratitude letters is another profound way to express this feeling. Taking the time to express, in words, how someone has positively impacted your life not only strengthens the bond with that person, but also provides a sense of connection and personal fulfillment. This practice transforms the simple act of thanking into a gift that deeply touches the recipient.

Thus, gratitude transcends the simple recognition of what is positive; it becomes a lifestyle, a constant posture of valuing the present. With each new opportunity recognized and appreciated, more space is created for the manifestation of new dreams and achievements. Like the glass of water that, when carefully balanced, can receive more without overflowing, life, when lived with gratitude, expands harmoniously, welcoming with lightness and fullness all that the universe has to offer.

When gratitude becomes an integral part of life, every experience, whether challenging or pleasurable, is perceived as an opportunity for learning and growth. This attentive and appreciative gaze transforms the way we interact with the world, making us more open, resilient, and empathetic. By recognizing the value of each moment, we begin to live with more purpose, connecting with what truly matters and moving away from unnecessary worries. This state of awareness leads us to a fuller existence, where the simple act of giving thanks is reflected in more positive and constructive attitudes.

This continuous flow of gratitude not only enriches one's own journey, but also positively influences those around us. Small gestures of recognition have the power to inspire and transform environments, creating a network of positive energy that expands naturally. By expressing gratitude, we contribute to building stronger and more authentic relationships, fostering cooperation, mutual respect, and collective growth. Thus, the practice of gratitude transcends the individual and becomes a force for social transformation, capable of generating a positive impact in different spheres of life.

Understanding gratitude as a continuous path and not as a final destination allows us to keep our hearts open to new experiences and learning. This constant movement of recognizing and valuing each stage of life strengthens us in the face of uncertainties and drives us to move forward with lightness and confidence. By cultivating this attitude daily, we become co-creators of a more harmonious and meaningful reality, where each step taken is celebrated and each achievement, big or small, is received with a sincere feeling of appreciation.

Chapter 27
Visualizing the Future

Visualizing the future is about consciously directing your mind to build your desired reality with clarity and purpose. It involves mentally creating concrete and inspiring scenarios where every detail reflects the goals you seek to achieve. This process doesn't depend solely on imagination, but on the ability to connect thoughts, emotions, and actions in a harmony that drives personal and professional fulfillment. By developing a clear and engaging vision of what you want to achieve, your mind naturally aligns with attitudes and decisions that favor the realization of these plans. Thus, visualization ceases to be a mere mental exercise and becomes a practical tool for transforming intentions into tangible results.

This method strengthens self-confidence and determination, allowing goals to be set with greater precision and obstacles to be faced with resilience. When the mind is trained to focus on future achievements, each step taken in the present gains more meaning and direction. This clarity of purpose eliminates distractions and enhances the ability to identify opportunities, facilitating strategic decision-making. The connection between positive thinking and consistent action creates an internal environment conducive to personal growth, motivating the constant pursuit of evolution and improvement.

By integrating visualization into everyday life, one begins to cultivate a mindset of abundance and prosperity. This internal alignment favors the attraction of resources, people, and circumstances that collaborate towards the achievement of objectives. The continuous practice of this process strengthens commitment to one's own dreams, increasing motivation and energy to overcome challenges. Thus, visualization becomes a powerful foundation for building a fulfilling life, guided by clear intentions, focus, and actions aligned with success and personal fulfillment.

Imagine an architect facing a blank sheet of paper. Before any lines are sketched, he already sees, in his mind, the finished building. Every detail—from the structural lines to the chosen materials, from the windows that capture the light to the interior design—takes shape with clarity. Nothing is left to chance. This complete visualization guides all stages of construction, ensuring that the final result is faithful to his initial conception. Similarly, by visualizing your future, you become the architect of your own life, designing with clarity and intention every aspect of the reality you wish to experience. With each detailed mental image, you build the foundation for a solid future, guided by purpose and determination.

Just as an architect needs a well-defined plan to materialize his work, visualizing the future allows you to transform abstract desires into concrete objectives.

This clarity is essential to establish priorities and chart viable paths to reach goals. When you can visualize with a wealth of detail what you want to achieve, decisions become more strategic, actions more focused, and opportunities become easier to recognize. This process not only organizes thoughts but also awakens the motivation needed to act with focus and persistence, making the journey more fluid and efficient.

This continuous practice of visualizing the future fuels genuine motivation. By imagining yourself living your ideal life, this mental image functions as emotional fuel. The enthusiasm generated by this projection drives action, maintaining focus even in the face of challenges. Each difficulty becomes a step, and each obstacle an opportunity for growth. The mind, nourished by these positive images, begins to operate in sync with the established goals, creating a cycle of constant and lasting motivation.

More than motivation, visualization strengthens the belief in achievement. When you see yourself reaching your goals, you mentally experience the feeling of victory, reducing doubts and insecurities. This symbolic experience of achievement creates a solid foundation of self-confidence. The mind begins to believe, with conviction, that these goals are possible and accessible. With this, you act with more courage and determination, moving firmly towards your dreams.

This connection between thought and reality also involves an energetic alignment. Frequently visualizing what you desire attracts circumstances, resources, and people that favor the achievement of these goals. It's like adjusting a radio frequency until you capture the perfect signal: thoughts and emotions come into harmony with the vibration of what you want to manifest. Thus, the environment around you begins to reflect this new harmony, making the process of realization more natural and spontaneous.

For visualization to be effective, it is necessary to create a conducive environment. Finding a quiet place where the mind can relax without interruption is the first step. It can be a quiet corner of the house, an outdoor space, or any place that inspires calm. In this environment, the body relaxes, breathing deepens, and the mind is freed from distractions. This state of serenity paves the way for the imagination to flow vividly and engagingly.

Setting clear and specific goals is also essential. Reflecting deeply on what you truly want to achieve helps align dreams with personal values. It's important to be detailed: how do you see yourself professionally? What kind of relationships do you want to cultivate? What lifestyle do you aspire to? The more precise this panorama, the stronger the impact of visualization. Clear goals become detailed maps, guiding each step towards fulfillment.

During this process, creating vivid mental images is fundamental. It is not enough to imagine superficially. It is necessary to visualize with a wealth of detail: the surrounding environment, the colors, the sounds, the aromas, and even the tactile sensations. Imagine how you move in this space, how you interact with people, how you react to situations. This intense mental experience activates the subconscious and stimulates creativity, making the transformation of these images into reality more tangible.

More than seeing, it is necessary to feel. Connecting with the emotions that accompany the achievement of your goals intensifies the impact of visualization. Experience the joy of achievement, gratitude for each step forward, the peace of being on the right path. These emotions raise the energetic vibration, deepening the connection between mind and universe. By feeling worthy of these achievements, you create an internal environment conducive to their manifestation.

Positive affirmations complement this process. Repeating phrases that reinforce confidence in one's own dreams consolidates the connection between thought and action. Phrases like "I am fully capable of achieving my goals" or "My life is in constant evolution and prosperity" should be said with conviction. This practice not only fuels self-confidence but also maintains focus and determination.

Gratitude also plays an essential role. Giving thanks as if your goals have already been achieved strengthens the positive vibration and attracts even more opportunities. This sincere feeling of gratitude establishes a bridge between the present and the desired future, expanding the connection with the universe and creating a constant flow of abundance.

For all these steps to be effective, visualization must become a constant habit. Setting aside daily or weekly moments to revisit your goals and enrich your mental images strengthens the manifestation process. Consistency engraves these visions in the subconscious, accelerating the path to fulfillment. Over time, this mental exercise becomes a natural tool for attracting and realizing your dreams.

Visualizing the future is, therefore, a conscious construction of every detail of the life you want to live. Just as an architect reviews and refines his project before starting construction, constantly visualizing your goals allows you to adjust plans, strengthen intentions, and move forward with confidence. The continuous practice of aligning thoughts, emotions, and actions creates a solid foundation for turning dreams into reality.

By allowing yourself to dream with clarity and intention, you place yourself in the position of co-creator of your own life. Each intentional thought guides your daily choices, making the path to fulfillment clearer and more accessible. Obstacles cease to be barriers and become opportunities for learning and evolution. Small daily steps, guided by this clear vision, translate into great achievements.

Therefore, by integrating visualization into your routine, you build a solid foundation for success and fulfillment. Each thought nurtured with purpose transforms into concrete action, and each action aligned with your purpose brings you closer to your desired future. Trust in the power of your mind and move forward with confidence, for with each visualization, the future you dream of is already beginning to take shape within you.

By incorporating visualization as an essential part of your routine, you establish a deep connection between your desires and your daily actions. Each intentional thought begins to positively influence your choices, making the path to fulfillment clearer and more accessible. This continuous practice not only fuels your motivation but also strengthens your resilience in the face of challenges, allowing you to view obstacles as opportunities for growth and learning. Thus, visualization naturally integrates into your evolution process, guiding your steps with confidence and purpose.

Over time, the results of this practice begin to manifest concretely in different areas of life. Small daily achievements turn into major advances, reinforcing the certainty that your dreams are possible and tangible. The clarity of your goals attracts opportunities aligned with your values and strengthens connections with people who share the same purposes. This constant flow of growth demonstrates that visualization is not just a mental exercise, but a bridge between intention and realization.

Therefore, by visualizing the future with detail and emotion, you build a solid foundation for success and fulfillment. Each thought cultivated with intention transforms into action, and each action aligned with your purpose contributes to the creation of your desired reality. Allow yourself to believe in the power of your mind and move forward with confidence, knowing that each step taken today brings you closer to the future that has already begun to be shaped within you.

Chapter 28
Acting with Intuition

Intuition represents a form of inner wisdom deeply connected to the essence of each individual. It arises as a subtle yet powerful perception, capable of guiding decisions, protecting against adversity, and pointing out promising opportunities. By trusting this inner guide, choices become more authentic and aligned with personal values, allowing life to flow in a more harmonious and meaningful way. This process involves recognizing and valuing the signals that the body and mind capture almost imperceptibly, integrating experiences and knowledge that go beyond rational logic. Thus, acting with intuition means allowing this natural wisdom to positively influence the paths taken, promoting balance and clarity in everyday decisions.

This connection with intuition strengthens self-confidence, since each successful decision reinforces the belief in one's own perceptions and instincts. Over time, this constant practice develops a keen ability to discern favorable and unfavorable situations, creating a positive cycle of trust and assertiveness. Intuition also expands the perception of opportunities, awakening the sensitivity to identify decisive moments that can be determinant for personal and professional growth. This alignment with one's own essence facilitates choices more consistent with goals and purposes, leading to a fuller and more abundant life.

Cultivating intuition requires dedication and openness to listening to one's own inner voice. Practices such as meditation, moments of silence and reflection, in addition to careful observation of sensations and emotions, are fundamental to strengthening this connection. By integrating these practices into everyday life, it becomes possible to access a deep wisdom that guides with clarity, even in the face of uncertainty. Trusting this process is essential to act with more security and authenticity, allowing intuition to become a powerful tool to transform challenges into opportunities and build a path of achievements aligned with the true purpose of life.

Imagine a lone sailor on the high seas, surrounded by dense fog. With no visible instruments to guide him, he turns to the hidden stars and a silent instinct that pulses within him. This navigator trusts in something beyond reason—an invisible compass that leads him back home. Such is intuition: an inner beacon that illuminates paths even in the most uncertain situations, guiding decisions that resonate with our deepest values, our dreams, and the purpose that gives meaning to life.

This inner wisdom acts as a direct bridge to the vast knowledge stored in the subconscious, integrating experiences, emotions, and learning in ways that rational logic often cannot reach. When we allow ourselves to listen to this inner voice, we access a source of authentic guidance, capable of aligning our choices with who we truly are. Like a persistent whisper, intuition guides us to recognize more coherent paths, removing distractions and leading us safely towards a fuller and more abundant life.

By following this inner guide, we develop the ability to make more assertive choices, avoiding detours that would take us away from our goals. Intuition presents itself as a natural filter, highlighting opportunities aligned with our purposes and warning about paths that may not be favorable. Each successful decision made based on this perception reinforces self-confidence and creates a virtuous cycle of trust and assertiveness. This expanded confidence drives us to act with more courage, even in the face of the unknown, transforming challenges into steps for personal and professional growth.

Furthermore, intuition plays a fundamental role in protecting against adverse situations. Small discomforts, inexplicable sensations, or subtle warnings can be signs that something is not right. Respecting these signs is a form of self-preservation, avoiding unnecessary risks and moving away from environments or people that may be harmful. This protective instinct often acts faster than any logical analysis, preserving emotional and physical balance.

But intuition not only warns of danger; it also opens doors to opportunities. Like a sensitive radar, it captures promising possibilities even before they become evident. This early perception allows us to be prepared to act at the right time, taking advantage of unique occasions that might otherwise go unnoticed.

Trusting these insights puts us in a position of advantage, allowing decisions to be made with confidence and agility.

Cultivating intuition, however, requires practice and surrender. The mind, often saturated with external stimuli, needs moments of silence and introspection to hear the inner voice. Practices such as meditation, mindful breathing, and reflection are essential to calm the mind and create space for intuition to manifest clearly. By slowing down the flow of thoughts, we open the way to perceive more clearly the answers that already inhabit us.

Observing the body's signals is also fundamental. Intuition communicates through subtle physical sensations—a tightness in the chest, a sinking feeling in the stomach, or a slight tension in the shoulders. Sudden emotions, spontaneous ideas, and recurring coincidences are manifestations of this inner wisdom. Paying attention to these signs and interpreting their meaning strengthens the connection with intuition and expands the perception of the world around.

When strong hunches or inexplicable impulses arise, it is important to trust these instincts, even if they do not make immediate sense. Often, intuition indicates paths that reason does not understand at the moment, but which prove to be correct over time. This act of trusting is a surrender to the natural flow of life, allowing choices to be guided not only by logic, but by the deep wisdom that dwells within us.

Recording these insights, thoughts, and dreams in a journal can be a powerful tool. By writing down intuitive perceptions, patterns begin to emerge, making it easier to understand how intuition manifests itself. This writing habit not only organizes thoughts, but also reinforces confidence in one's own instincts, making them more accessible and clear in everyday life.

In moments of decision, especially those with great impact, taking a moment to listen to one's own intuition can reveal more authentic answers. Important decisions, such as career changes, financial investments, or new relationships, can be better managed when aligned with this inner knowing. Intuition offers a unique perspective, often revealing creative solutions or preventing hasty choices.

In relationships, intuition acts as an emotional radar. It identifies subtleties in people's behavior, allowing you to discern who truly contributes to our growth and who may represent an obstacle. Trusting this discernment is essential to build healthy and harmonious bonds, surrounding yourself with people who share positive energies and aligned purposes.

In the financial field, intuition complements rational analysis. When considering investments or business decisions, perceiving internal signals that suggest caution or enthusiasm can be decisive. This balance between logic and intuition avoids unnecessary risks and highlights lucrative opportunities that might otherwise go unnoticed.

Creativity also flourishes under the influence of intuition. Ideas that arise spontaneously, without logical explanation, can be sources of innovation and originality. Allowing yourself to explore these ideas, even if they initially seem disconnected, opens the way to authentic creations that reflect the essence of who we are. Intuition, in this context, is an inexhaustible source of inspiration.

To strengthen this ability, it is essential to cultivate self-confidence. Believing in one's own perceptions and validating the signals that arise is the first step. The constant practice of trusting intuition, even in the face of uncertainty, develops a deeper relationship with one's own inner voice, making it a constant ally in everyday decisions.

It is also important to be patient. The development of intuition is a gradual process that strengthens over time and experience. Daily self-knowledge practices, such as meditation and reflection, refine the sensitivity to capture subtle signals. Respecting this rhythm of growth and trusting the process is fundamental for intuition to become a safe guide.

And, above all, it is necessary not to fear mistakes. Not all intuitive decisions will be correct, but each experience, whether successful or not, brings valuable lessons. Accepting mistakes as part of the path strengthens the confidence to act intuitively, without the weight of self-criticism, and expands the ability to interpret signals more clearly.

Connecting with nature is another powerful way to nurture intuition. The simplicity and silence of natural environments calm the mind and expand perception. Outdoor walks, moments of contemplation, or simply listening to the sound of the wind and water are practices that restore balance and deepen the connection with inner wisdom.

Acting with intuition is, therefore, allowing yourself to live with more authenticity and presence. It is trusting that life offers subtle answers, and that each choice guided by this inner knowing builds a more coherent and meaningful path. By honoring this silent voice, we transform challenges into opportunities and shape a truer, fuller life aligned with who we truly are.

By consciously integrating intuition into your routine, it becomes possible to navigate life's challenges with more lightness. This deep connection with inner wisdom does not eliminate difficulties, but it offers clarity to face them with balance and authenticity. Over time, the constant practice of listening to and respecting one's own inner signals transforms the way one deals with choices and unforeseen events, allowing each step to be taken with more confidence and purpose.

This alignment with intuition not only strengthens self-confidence, but also promotes a more harmonious relationship with the world around. By perceiving the subtleties of situations and people, a space of respect and mutual understanding is created, facilitating genuine connections and more accurate decisions. Intuition becomes a link between reason and feeling, guiding with sensitivity and firmness towards paths that favor personal and collective growth.

Thus, acting with intuition is an invitation to live more presently and connected with one's own essence. It is allowing oneself to trust in the flow of life, recognizing that each choice, guided by this inner knowing, contributes to the construction of a more authentic and fulfilling journey. By valuing this subtle voice that inhabits the intimate, space is opened to live with more truth, courage, and purpose, transforming challenges into opportunities and dreams into reality.

Chapter 29
Spiritual Connection

Spiritual connection represents a deep and essential link with a higher power, capable of nourishing the soul and illuminating the path of life with purpose and balance. This connection transcends rational understanding, awakening a genuine sense of belonging to the universe and revealing the harmony between the human being and the divine. By strengthening this bond, it becomes possible to access an inexhaustible source of love, wisdom and inner strength, which guides decisions, inspires actions and promotes personal growth. This state of connection broadens the perception that each experience has a purpose and that life flows in perfect synchronicity with a higher order.

This spiritual integration elevates consciousness, allowing emotions such as gratitude, compassion and inner peace to manifest naturally. Alignment with this higher energy awakens a state of balance and serenity, making challenges lighter and achievements more meaningful. This inner harmony not only strengthens faith in oneself and in life, but also creates space to recognize and attract opportunities for growth and prosperity. Spirituality, when cultivated with authenticity, transforms the way one perceives the world, promoting a fuller existence aligned with one's true purpose.

To deepen this connection, it is essential to adopt practices that integrate body, mind and spirit, allowing the flourishing of a higher consciousness. Meditation, prayer, contact with nature and continuous reflection are effective ways to silence external noise and listen to the inner voice. Through these practices, one develops the ability to interpret the signs of life with clarity, make wiser decisions and act with confidence. By establishing this intimate relationship with the divine, it becomes possible to access an abundance that manifests itself in all areas of life, creating a journey guided by love, harmony and true well-being.

Imagine a robust tree, whose deep roots extend through the soil, absorbing vital nutrients and offering support. Just as this tree nourishes itself from the earth to grow and flourish, spiritual connection is the invisible foundation that unites us to a source of greater energy, supplying us with strength, wisdom and balance. This connection with the divine strengthens us in the face of challenges and allows us to flourish in all areas of life.

This spiritual connection is not just an abstract idea, but a profound experience that fills the soul with purpose and meaning. By recognizing this greater force, we awaken to the understanding that every event, however simple or challenging, carries a purpose. We begin to perceive that life follows a flow in perfect harmony with a higher order, where everything happens at the right time for our growth and evolution. This awareness brings us serenity to accept what we cannot control and courage to act when necessary.

Being spiritually connected raises our vibration and puts us in tune with genuine feelings of love, gratitude, compassion and inner peace. This alignment not only softens daily challenges, but also expands our ability to celebrate achievements with humility and joy. When we vibrate at this high frequency, we naturally attract positive experiences and opportunities that contribute to our development. Spirituality, when lived authentically, transforms our way of seeing the world and allows us to live with more lightness, purpose and fulfillment.

This spiritual integration also strengthens faith - not just as a belief in something greater, but as an unshakeable trust that we are being guided and supported. Faith gives us the security to move forward, even in the face of adversity. It reminds us that although we cannot foresee the entire path, we can trust the next step. With this trust, decisions become clearer, and challenges are faced with courage and resilience.

Furthermore, spiritual connection awakens intuition, that subtle voice that guides us with wisdom and clarity. By silencing the mind and listening to this inner guidance, we make decisions that are more aligned with our values and life purpose. This attentive listening protects us from impulsive choices and guides us towards paths that truly contribute to our evolution. Intuition, strengthened by spirituality, functions as a compass that directs us with safety and lightness.

Another fundamental aspect of this connection is the awakening of life purpose. Often, the search for meaning is lost amidst external pressures and expectations. However, by strengthening the bond with the divine, we are led to a deeper understanding of who we are and what we have come to accomplish. This purpose, when identified, drives us with genuine motivation, making each action more meaningful and aligned with our deepest values.

Gratitude also flourishes naturally in this state of connection. By recognizing daily blessings, small or large, we create space for more abundance to manifest. Gratitude transforms the way we perceive life, allowing us to focus on the gifts we have already received, which in turn attracts new opportunities and positive experiences. This virtuous cycle of gratitude and abundance leads us on a journey of constant fulfillment.

Compassion emerges as another fruit of this spiritual connection. By feeling part of something greater, we develop empathy not only for ourselves, but for all beings. This understanding invites us to act with more kindness, patience and love, contributing to healthier relationships and a more harmonious living environment. Compassion, when cultivated, strengthens human bonds and promotes a sense of unity and solidarity.

To deepen this connection, daily practices are essential. Meditation, for example, leads us to inner silence, allowing the mind to calm down and inner wisdom to emerge. This constant habit expands our perception and strengthens the relationship with the divine, creating a sense of peace and balance. Meditation teaches us to inhabit the present and listen to the whispers of the soul.

Prayer also stands out as a powerful tool for connection. More than words, prayer is an intimate dialogue with the sacred, where we express gratitude, seek guidance and renew our faith. This practice reminds us that we are not alone and offers us comfort and strength in times of uncertainty.

Physical practices, such as yoga, complement this process. Yoga integrates body, mind and spirit through conscious movement, breathing and meditation. This alignment promotes physical well-being, mental clarity and spiritual expansion, establishing a deep connection with our essence. The body comes to be recognized as a sacred temple, deserving of care and respect.

Contact with nature is also one of the simplest and most effective ways to reconnect with the divine. Observing the movement of trees, listening to the singing of birds or feeling the breeze on your face are experiences that remind us of the grandeur of creation. Being in the midst of nature reminds us of the simplicity and beauty of life, renewing our energies and bringing us back to our center.

Studying sacred texts is another way to expand spiritual understanding. The scriptures offer profound and timeless teachings that illuminate the path with wisdom. Reflecting on these messages allows us to integrate spiritual values into our daily decisions and actions, guiding us with ethics and compassion.

Charity and acts of kindness are also practical manifestations of spirituality. By extending a hand to others, we share divine love and contribute to the collective good. Helping others, whether with words of support or concrete actions, strengthens our connection with the essence of life and allows us to experience true abundance.

Forgiveness presents itself as an essential practice for inner peace. Freeing ourselves from hurt and resentment aligns us with the energy of love and allows us to move forward with lightness. Forgiveness, whether to ourselves or to others, dissolves emotional blocks and opens space for healing and renewal.

Finally, self-knowledge is the path that integrates all these practices. Knowing oneself deeply is essential to live with authenticity and fullness. This inner journey reveals our values, limits and potentials, allowing our choices to be aligned with our divine purpose. Self-knowledge illuminates the path to a more conscious and abundant life.

When spiritual connection becomes part of our daily lives, all areas of life are transformed. Financial prosperity flows in a balanced way, emotions stabilize, the mind becomes clear and creative, the body gains vitality and the spirit expands. This state of fullness reflects a life lived with meaning, guided by wisdom and love.

Thus, cultivating spiritual connection is allowing life to unfold in harmony with the universe. It is trusting that each step leads us to a more authentic and meaningful existence. When we surrender to this connection, we flourish like the deep-rooted tree: firm, nourished and ready to reach for the sky.

When spiritual connection becomes an integral part of life, each experience gains a deeper and more conscious meaning. Difficulties are seen as opportunities for growth and learning, while achievements are celebrated with gratitude and humility. This state of presence and alignment with the divine strengthens trust in the natural flow of life, allowing challenges to be faced with serenity and victories to be appreciated as a reflection of a greater purpose being fulfilled.

This intimate relationship with the sacred also expands compassion and empathy, not only with oneself, but with all beings. The understanding that everything is interconnected awakens a sense of collective responsibility, inspiring more conscious and harmonious attitudes. Thus, spiritual connection transcends the individual sphere and extends to the world around, promoting balance, respect and love in each interaction, contributing to a more peaceful and collaborative environment.

By cultivating this continuous connection with the divine, life is transformed into a journey of fulfillment, purpose and abundance. The path becomes lighter, guided by inner wisdom and trust in the universe. Each step is taken with more awareness, each decision reflects the authenticity of being, and each moment is lived with depth. Thus, spiritual connection not only illuminates the path, but also strengthens the roots, allowing you to flourish with love, wisdom and true peace.

Chapter 30
Serving the World

Serving the world represents a genuine commitment to using talents, skills and passions to generate a positive impact and contribute to the collective good. This attitude transcends individual interests and manifests itself through concrete actions that promote social, environmental and human transformation. Each gesture of generosity and solidarity strengthens the construction of a more just, inclusive and sustainable society, demonstrating that true abundance multiplies when shared. The connection with this purpose raises awareness and awakens the responsibility to actively act in improving the world, creating a continuous cycle of personal and collective growth.

By directing efforts towards meaningful causes, it is possible to positively influence the lives of others and strengthen human bonds. Engagement in social, environmental or educational actions broadens the understanding of the world's needs and reinforces the importance of empathy, respect and cooperation. This stance inspires attitudes of compassion and responsibility, cultivating an environment where everyone can thrive. Thus, serving the world becomes an opportunity to align personal values with practical actions, creating real impacts that reverberate in various spheres of society.

This journey of service to others not only benefits the community, but also provides a deep sense of fulfillment and purpose. Involvement in noble causes strengthens self-esteem, develops interpersonal skills and expands support networks. Each contribution, however small it may seem, is a seed planted for a more harmonious and abundant future. Serving the world is, therefore, a path of mutual transformation, where those who offer also receive, experiencing the fullness that arises from making a difference in the lives of others.

Imagine a dedicated gardener who lovingly cares for his own garden, but is not content to keep the beauty just for himself. He shares his flowers, his fruits and even his seeds with the community around him. This act of generosity spreads colors, aromas and life, making the collective environment more beautiful and welcoming. Serving the world is like being this gardener: cultivating good with our talents and sharing what we have best to flourish the lives of everyone around us.

When we put our gifts and abilities at the service of the collective good, we connect deeply with the true purpose of existence. This surrender transcends personal interests and aligns us with something greater, promoting impacts that reverberate in various spheres of society. Serving the world does not just mean great deeds; it also involves small daily gestures of empathy, generosity and solidarity. Each positive action, however small it may seem, is a planted seed that germinates into social, environmental and human transformation.

This attitude of service expands our consciousness and connects us directly with the abundance of life. By acting with love, compassion and gratitude, we raise our vibration and attract positive experiences. This state of energetic alignment not only strengthens inner balance, but also opens paths to new opportunities. Life becomes lighter and more fluid, as the energy we donate returns multiplied. The act of serving, therefore, is not a sacrifice, but a two-way street: while we offer, we also receive.

Furthermore, dedicating oneself to others strengthens self-esteem and a sense of belonging. By realizing that our actions positively impact other people, we feel a deep sense of accomplishment. This feeling of usefulness and purpose empowers us, encouraging us to continue contributing. It is a virtuous cycle where the act of giving becomes a source of motivation, joy and personal growth.

To walk this path of service with authenticity, it is essential to identify our passions and talents. Each person has unique skills that can be applied in a practical and transformative way. Whether teaching, creating, organizing or supporting, there is always a way to contribute. When we direct our gifts to causes that inspire us, our impact becomes even more meaningful and sustainable.

Finding volunteer opportunities is a direct way to put this purpose into practice. Participating in social, environmental or educational projects brings us closer to the realities that most need attention. Involvement in concrete actions strengthens community ties, expands our worldview and connects us with people who share the same values.

Another way to serve is through conscious donation. Contributing financially to institutions and projects aligned with our principles is an effective way to support initiatives that promote real change. More than the material value, it is the gesture of commitment to the collective good that generates impact. Small contributions, added to many others, have the power to transform lives.

Sharing knowledge and experiences is also a powerful way to serve. Offering mentoring, lectures or workshops allows other people to have access to tools and information that can open doors to new opportunities. This exchange of knowledge multiplies the positive impact and encourages the personal and professional growth of those seeking evolution.

Practicing conscious consumption is equally important. Choosing to support companies and products that respect the environment, promote social justice and adopt ethical practices reinforces collective responsibility. Our consumption choices directly influence the world around us and can be a form of service when guided by principles of sustainability and ethics.

Being an agent of change starts with daily attitudes. A simple gesture of kindness, a word of encouragement or an action of respect for others has the power to inspire great transformations. Small attitudes, when practiced consistently, create a culture of care and solidarity that spreads and motivates others to also act for the common good.

There are several areas in which we can serve the world. In the environment, we can participate in preservation initiatives, such as planting trees or recycling campaigns. In education, supporting literacy projects or mentoring can be a key to reducing inequalities. In health, volunteering in hospitals and support homes brings comfort and hope to those who need it most. In the fight against poverty, donating food, clothing and time helps to minimize difficulties. In the defense of human rights, fighting discrimination and promoting equality builds a more just and safe society.

To effectively serve the world, you don't need to start with big projects. Small steps are of great value. A simple gesture of affection can be the beginning of a transformative impact. By identifying the causes that touch us deeply, our involvement becomes more authentic and persistent. Consistency in actions is fundamental to generate real and sustainable changes.

Teamwork further enhances this impact. By joining forces with other people who share the same ideals, we create stronger and more comprehensive movements. Together, we overcome challenges and achieve results that, individually, would be limited. Cooperation expands the scope of actions and strengthens the spirit of community.

Recognizing and celebrating every small achievement along the way is essential. Valuing progress, however small, fuels motivation and inspires others to follow the same path. Building a better world doesn't happen overnight, but every step is essential. Celebrating these steps reminds us that we are moving forward and makes the journey even more rewarding.

Serving the world is also a journey of self-discovery. Each experience lived in this process reveals new perspectives, deepens our values and strengthens our hope for a more just and compassionate future. Sincere surrender transforms not only those who are helped, but also those who help. This continuous cycle of giving and receiving nourishes the soul and generates a deep sense of belonging.

By putting our talents and resources at the service of the collective good, we leave a legacy of love, respect and solidarity. Each positive action is a planted seed that will flourish into new fruits of hope and harmony. Thus, serving the world becomes a path of personal and collective fulfillment, where everyone leaves transformed and enriched.

Therefore, being like the gardener who shares his flowers and seeds is understanding that true growth happens when our actions flourish in the lives of others. When we choose to serve, we not only help transform the world, but we also transform ourselves, discovering the true essence of abundance and fulfillment.

Serving the world is a constant invitation to reflect on the role that each individual plays in building a more balanced and harmonious future. This commitment does not require grand gestures to be meaningful; often, it is the simple and authentic attitudes that most touch and transform lives. The impact generated by a word of encouragement, a welcoming smile or a gesture of sincere support is immeasurable, as it reverberates positively in human relations and inspires silent but profound changes. Thus, each person has the ability to become an agent of transformation, contributing what they have most valuable: their humanity.

By embracing this journey of service, one realizes that true power lies in collaboration and collective spirit. The union of individual efforts creates great movements, capable of overcoming complex challenges and promoting significant advances in various areas. When talents, resources and intentions converge for the common good, solidarity networks are formed that strengthen communities and expand the scope of actions. This shared path reinforces the notion that no one is alone in the mission to improve the world and that, together, we are stronger and more effective.

Finally, serving the world is also a process of self-discovery and evolution. Each experience lived in this genuine surrender reveals new perspectives, strengthens essential values and nourishes the hope of a more compassionate and just future. This virtuous cycle of giving and receiving transforms not only those who are helped, but also those who help, awakening a deep sense of belonging and purpose. Thus, by putting the heart and talents at the service of the collective good, a lasting legacy is built, where each positive action is a seed that will flourish into new opportunities for growth and harmony for all.

Chapter 31
Following your Intuition

Intuition emerges as an essential and reliable tool to guide decisions and choices throughout life. It represents a natural wisdom, deeply rooted in personal experience and accumulated knowledge, capable of indicating paths that lead to growth, well-being, and fulfillment. Trusting this inner sense means recognizing and valuing the subtle signs that manifest through sensations, perceptions, and spontaneous thoughts. This process involves attentive listening and a genuine connection with one's own essence, allowing decisions to be made more authentically and aligned with true personal desires and purposes. When one learns to respect and follow these internal directions, space is opened to experience more satisfying experiences, healthier relationships, and opportunities that drive development in various areas of life.

By strengthening the connection with intuition, it becomes possible to perceive opportunities that were previously unnoticed, avoiding pitfalls and identifying more clearly the best paths to follow. This heightened perception contributes to more assertive choices, both professionally and in interpersonal relationships and in managing daily challenges. Intuition acts as a silent beacon, illuminating paths that are often not immediately obvious to logic, but which lead to positive and enriching results. Developing this sensitivity implies cultivating moments of reflection, silencing the mind in the face of external noise, and trusting one's own perceptions, even when they seem to contradict rational patterns. This continuous practice of self-knowledge and self-confidence allows one to build a solid foundation for decisions that are more consistent with personal goals.

Furthermore, integrating intuition into everyday life increases self-confidence and the ability to act decisively in the face of challenges. This inner strength, when recognized and respected, promotes emotional balance and mental clarity, fundamental to facing changes and uncertainties with greater security. Intuition, therefore, is not just a sporadic resource, but a natural ability that can be constantly improved. By trusting this instinct, harmony is created between reason and feeling, allowing each step to be taken with conviction and authenticity. This conscious integration of intuition into daily decisions opens doors to a fuller, more balanced life, aligned with the true purpose of each individual.

Imagine a lone explorer diving into a dense and unknown forest. Without a map or physical compass, he advances trusting only his deepest instincts. Every sound, every movement of the leaves, and every subtle change in wind direction become silent signals, guiding his steps. This explorer carefully observes the almost invisible trails, notices the birdsong that indicates hidden dangers, and senses the presence of safe paths in the air. There is no guarantee that every decision will lead him directly to the desired destination, but he understands that there is wisdom in every instinctive choice. Thus, the forest, once intimidating, reveals itself as a territory of possibilities, where trust in one's own perception opens space for valuable discoveries and learning. Following intuition is exactly like being this explorer, navigating the uncertainties of life with courage and confidence in an internal compass that, silent and firm, indicates the way forward.

This same intuition acts as a bridge between the individual and abundance in all areas of life. By connecting with your inner truth, it becomes possible to access authentic desires, genuine passions, and talents that often remain dormant under external pressures. This deep self-knowledge directs choices more aligned with who you truly are, leading to paths that favor personal and professional fulfillment. When you listen to this inner voice, decisions are made with greater clarity and coherence, bringing each step closer to your life purpose. Intuition, subtle but powerful, indicates opportunities that resonate with personal growth and flourishing, guiding you towards experiences that enrich and expand your perception of abundance.

In addition to guiding you in the right direction, intuition functions as a protective shield. It perceives dangers long before they become apparent, picking up signals invisible to the naked eye. This subtle hunch warns of potentially harmful people and situations, avoiding pitfalls and preventing impulsive choices. This silent protection is not the result of paranoia, but of an inner wisdom that interprets nuances and signals with a precision that logic often does not achieve. By trusting this sensitivity, decisions become safer and more conscious, allowing you to navigate life with more lightness and confidence.

Intuition also has the power to open doors that, at first glance, might go unnoticed. Often, it inspires strategic moves and bold decisions at the right time, creating opportunities that can be decisive for success and complete fulfillment. This keen eye allows you to perceive hidden possibilities in the details and act with the conviction of someone who knows they are on the right path. Life, then, becomes a fertile field for the emergence of new ideas, projects, and relationships that drive prosperity in various areas.

Trusting your own intuition strengthens self-confidence in a profound and lasting way. This strengthening occurs because, by recognizing the value of one's own perceptions, an inner security emerges that removes doubts and uncertainties. Each decision made based on this inner confidence reinforces the ability to act authentically, allowing you to tread personal and unique paths. This empowerment is liberating, as it grants permission to live according to one's own values and dreams, creating the life that one truly wants to experience.

To cultivate this intuitive connection, it is essential to silence the noise of the mind. Intuition expresses itself subtly, so it is necessary to create moments of stillness so that this inner voice can be heard. Practices such as meditation, mindfulness, and breathing exercises are effective tools to calm thoughts and open space for clearer perceptions. In this mental tranquility, previously ignored signals become perceptible, allowing for decisions that are more aligned with your essence.

Being attentive to the signs is another fundamental step. Intuition manifests itself in different ways: physical sensations, sudden emotions, spontaneous thoughts, or even recurring dreams. Each sign carries a message that, when interpreted with sensitivity, guides choices and attitudes. Developing this listening requires practice and patience, but over time, it becomes natural to perceive and trust these alerts and directions.

Following your instincts, even if they contradict logic, is one of the most authentic ways to live. Often, reason will try to impose limitations, but intuition offers paths that, although challenging, lead to growth. Trusting this inner impulse is allowing yourself to go beyond the obvious and explore possibilities that the rational mind would not consider. This act of courage opens doors to enriching and transformative experiences.

Recording perceptions and insights is also a valuable practice. By writing down dreams, hunches, and synchronicities, a record is created that facilitates the identification of intuitive patterns. This habit strengthens trust in one's own intuition and allows one to recognize more clearly the signs that life offers.

In the work environment, for example, intuition can be decisive. It guides the choice of projects, indicates the best time for career changes, and reveals growth opportunities that are not always evident. In interpersonal relationships, this sensitivity helps to identify people who vibrate in tune with our values, facilitating the construction of healthy and lasting bonds. In finance, intuition guides decisions about investments and resource management, helping to perceive risks and opportunities before they materialize.

In the field of health, intuition plays a fundamental role in prevention and care. The body sends subtle signals about its physical and emotional state, and being attentive to these alerts can be decisive in maintaining balance and well-being. Intuition also guides choices of practices and treatments that resonate with individual needs, promoting a more integrated and conscious approach to health.

In spirituality, this inner connection leads to authentic paths of self-discovery and expansion of consciousness. Allowing yourself to explore different spiritual practices according to what makes sense personally strengthens the relationship with the sacred and with the purpose of life.

For intuition to fully flourish, you need to trust yourself. This trust is the solid foundation that supports inner listening. Being courageous to follow intuition, even in the face of uncertainty, is fundamental. Patience also plays an important role, as the development of intuition is a continuous process. Learning from mistakes and celebrating successes are attitudes that reinforce this connection, making intuition increasingly accurate and reliable.

When intuition is consciously cultivated, it transforms the way we deal with challenges and embrace opportunities. This attentive and respectful listening builds a solid foundation for wise decisions aligned with our values. Intuition does not eliminate obstacles, but it offers clarity to face them with lightness and assertiveness. This alignment between mind, body, and spirit strengthens serene confidence, guiding each step with authenticity. Thus, intuition becomes a bridge between the present and the desired future, leading to a fuller, more meaningful life in harmony with true purpose.

When intuition is consciously cultivated, it transforms the way we face challenges and embrace opportunities. This continuous process of inner listening and self-confidence becomes a solid foundation for wiser decisions that are more aligned with our values. Intuition does not eliminate obstacles from the path, but it offers clarity to deal with them more lightly and assertively. By realizing that this inner wisdom is a constant ally, a space is opened to act with more balance, allowing each choice to reflect who we truly are.

This deep alignment between mind, body, and spirit strengthens the ability to live authentically and resiliently. Decisions are no longer driven by fear or doubt and become guided by a serene confidence, capable of sustaining the journey even in the face of uncertainty. Thus, intuition is revealed as a link between the present and the desired future, facilitating the manifestation of more meaningful experiences aligned with personal dreams and goals.

By allowing intuition to guide each step, the journey becomes richer, full of learning and discovery. Each experience lived with this attentive listening reveals new possibilities and strengthens trust in the natural flow of life. This intuitive path is not linear, but it is full of meaning, leading to a fuller, more authentic existence in tune with true purpose.

Chapter 32
Living with Purpose

Living with purpose means leading one's life with clarity, direction, and meaning, where each choice and action is aligned with personal values and deeper aspirations. This way of living consciously integrates talents, passions, and skills, transforming challenges into opportunities for growth and progress. Life gains depth and authenticity when one recognizes the value of each experience and uses this learning to build a path that reflects one's essence. This alignment strengthens confidence, drives motivation, and opens space for a full and abundant journey, connecting each step taken to a greater meaning.

By integrating purpose and action, it becomes possible to transform dreams into concrete goals, guided by decisions consistent with one's own identity. This commitment to what truly matters brings clarity in the face of uncertainty and strengthens resilience in the face of challenges. The search for purpose involves self-knowledge and authenticity, allowing one to recognize one's own abilities and limitations, which leads to more conscious choices aligned with life goals. Thus, purpose acts as a driving force that guides daily attitudes, leading to meaningful results and continuous personal fulfillment.

This full experience also favors connection with the world around, inspiring positive contributions to society and strengthening human relationships based on empathy and collaboration. Living with purpose is not just about achieving goals, but about building a meaningful path that balances personal achievements with collective impact. The path becomes lighter and more satisfying when each decision reflects one's own values, creating a life rich in meaning and fulfillment. This integration between purpose and action not only strengthens self-confidence, but also attracts enriching opportunities and experiences, sustaining an authentic and truly abundant existence.

Imagine a river that flows firmly and clearly towards the sea. Its waters travel the path with determination, fed by rain, springs, and tributaries that join it along the journey. This river does not question its direction; it follows its course, diverting obstacles, adapting to the terrain, but always moving forward. Living with purpose is like being this river: flowing with direction and intentionality, driven by the force of one's own essence and guided by the wisdom of the heart. Just as the river finds its way even in the face of rocks and unexpected curves, life with purpose allows you to face challenges with resilience, transforming difficulties into opportunities for growth.

Having a purpose gives meaning to existence. It connects the person to something greater than themselves, awakening a profound reason to live and fight for their own dreams. This connection brings not only motivation, but also a sense of belonging to something great, encouraging the pursuit of a positive impact on the world. When one understands that there is a greater meaning behind daily actions, each step becomes more conscious and loaded with intention. Purpose transforms routine into a meaningful journey, where each challenge overcome and each achievement reached are essential parts of a path that is built with authenticity.

This purpose is also the force that drives action. It serves as an engine that moves the person to transform dreams into reality with enthusiasm and determination. In moments of doubt or difficulty, remembering why you started strengthens resilience and maintains focus. The path to achieving goals becomes clearer when you are aware of the why behind each choice. Motivation fueled by a genuine purpose is constant and resistant, allowing you to overcome obstacles with confidence, as there is clarity about the desired destination.

Living with purpose also serves as a guide in important life decisions. It acts as a filter, aligning choices with personal values and goals. This consistency avoids detours that could take the person away from what really matters. Decisions are made with more security and assertiveness, leading to paths that reflect true essence. This continuous guidance facilitates the search for abundance and fulfillment, creating a fuller and more connected life.

In addition to guiding actions, purpose reveals the abundance that already resides within each of us. When you live in alignment with your own talents, passions, and creativity, it becomes possible to recognize and use this inner strength fully. This awareness strengthens self-confidence, allowing authenticity to manifest itself in all areas of life. Inner abundance is the foundation that sustains outer prosperity, because by valuing what you already have, you create space to attract new opportunities.

This alignment between purpose and action also attracts external abundance. When actions are authentic and connected to life's mission, opportunities arise naturally. Life begins to flow with more lightness and synchronicity, creating prosperity in various areas, such as relationships, career, finances, health, and spirituality. The congruence between being and doing generates magnetism, attracting people and circumstances that contribute to personal and collective growth.

To find this purpose, it is essential to start a journey of self-knowledge. Reflecting on values, passions, talents, and skills allows you to understand what truly inspires and gives meaning to life. Questions like "What makes me feel alive?" and "What activities spark my enthusiasm?" are valuable starting points for discovering your essence. This inner dive reveals paths that resonate with authenticity and lead to a more meaningful life.

Recognizing your own values is equally essential. Knowing which principles guide actions and decisions allows you to make more consistent choices. Identifying what is non-negotiable strengthens personal integrity and avoids detours that could compromise authenticity.

This alignment with personal values ensures that each step is taken with conviction, contributing to the construction of a true path.

Reconnecting with your inner child can also be a key to discovering purpose. Remembering the activities that delighted you in childhood and the dreams that seemed grandiose can reveal genuine passions. Often, the purest interests manifest themselves early on and indicate natural talents that can be developed. This reconnection brings out a spontaneity that translates into more authentic and enjoyable choices.

Paying attention to your own interests and curiosities is another effective way to identify purpose. What arouses fascination and a desire to learn? What topics provoke enthusiasm? These clues indicate directions that make sense and can open doors to new opportunities. Following these interests with courage and curiosity leads to paths rich in meaning.

Trying new things broadens horizons and allows you to discover hidden talents. Exploring different environments, traveling, learning new skills, and stepping outside your comfort zone are ways to expand your worldview. Each experience lived brings learning that contributes to the construction of a richer and more authentic life. Experimentation opens space to discover unexpected passions and strengthens the ability to adapt.

Intuition also plays a fundamental role in this quest. It functions as an inner compass, guiding through sensations and insights that are not always understood by logic. Trusting this inner voice allows you to access a deep wisdom aligned with your own essence. This intuitive guidance reveals paths that lead to transformative and authentic experiences.

Reflecting on the impact you want to make on the world helps illuminate purpose. Questions like "What legacy do I want to leave?" or "How can I contribute to a better world?" encourage deep reflection on life's mission. This outward-looking perspective broadens the meaning of actions and strengthens commitment to something greater.

Being inspired by people who live with purpose can be motivating. Observing the trajectories of individuals who positively impact the world reveals possibilities and paths to follow. Identifying aspects of these stories that resonate with your own journey strengthens the motivation to act and transforms inspiration into concrete action.

It is important to remember that discovering purpose is an ongoing process. There's no rush. Patience with yourself is essential to allow this path to unfold gradually. Each experience lived contributes to the construction of a full and meaningful life. Constant action, even in small steps, is what allows you to live your purpose concretely.

Aligning actions with deep values is essential to living with purpose. Each decision must reflect principles that support personal integrity. Seeking balance between responsibilities, leisure, and personal growth maintains energy and motivation to move forward without neglecting well-being. Putting talents at the service of the collective amplifies the positive impact, strengthening the sense of accomplishment.

Practicing gratitude for each lesson and achievement along the journey reinforces the connection to purpose. Valuing small victories strengthens motivation and attracts new opportunities. Celebrating each achievement fuels confidence and maintains enthusiasm to move forward with determination.

Thus, living with purpose is a constant invitation to authenticity, courage, and conscious action. By aligning intentions, choices, and attitudes with one's own essence, one builds a life full of meaning. This path not only fulfills individually, but also inspires and transforms the world around.

Throughout this journey of self-discovery and fulfillment, it is essential to remember that purpose is not something fixed or unchanging. It evolves as we grow, mature, and gain new perspectives. Being open to change and adaptation allows purpose to be refined over time, becoming even more aligned with our essence. This dynamism is what keeps life vibrant and full of possibilities, providing space for new dreams, challenges, and achievements that enrich the path traveled.

Furthermore, cultivating presence in the present moment is fundamental to living with purpose. Often, we are so focused on future goals that we forget to value the present, where the most meaningful experiences happen. By practicing mindfulness, we are able to enjoy each stage of the journey, recognizing the small victories and lessons that sustain personal growth. This balance between future vision and appreciation of the present strengthens the connection to our life mission and drives us to move forward with lightness and confidence.

Finally, living with purpose is a constant invitation to authenticity and courage. It is allowing yourself to be true to yourself, honoring your own values and dreams, even in the face of uncertainty. Each step taken with intention strengthens the path, making it not just a trajectory of achievements, but also of deep meaning. By integrating purpose, action, and authenticity, we build a life that not only fulfills us individually, but also inspires and transforms the world around us.

Chapter 33
Material Detachment

Detaching from material possessions is an essential step towards achieving a lighter, fuller, and more meaningful life. By reducing the importance given to objects and possessions, we create the opportunity to value deeper aspects of existence, such as lived experiences, genuine relationships, and connection with our own essence. This process allows us to recognize that happiness is not linked to the accumulation of things, but to the ability to live with authenticity and purpose. Letting go of material excess is, therefore, a conscious choice that expands our perception of abundance, making life more balanced and satisfying.

By freeing ourselves from attachment to possessions, we create space for newness and personal growth. This space is not only physical, but also mental and emotional, allowing new opportunities, ideas, and relationships to develop naturally. The lightness achieved by getting rid of the superfluous makes it easier to focus on what really matters, promoting clarity in decisions and strengthening the ability to deal with everyday challenges. This transformation is profound because it directly impacts well-being, emotional health, and the way we see the world, contributing to a more conscious and fulfilling existence.

This change in perspective paves the way for a more authentic life, where the search for meaning replaces the need to accumulate goods. Material detachment strengthens the connection with essential values, such as gratitude, simplicity, and generosity, allowing true abundance to manifest in all areas of life. This new perspective provides freedom and autonomy, eliminating the anxiety generated by consumerism and creating an environment conducive to emotional balance and personal fulfillment. Thus, by prioritizing experiences and human connections, it becomes possible to live with more purpose, fully enjoying each moment.

Imagine a bird soaring high in the sky, gliding smoothly through the wind, carrying nothing but its own wings. It does not accumulate possessions, nor does it build up reserves of weight that could limit its flight. The bird follows light and free, guided only by instinct and the essential need to exist. Material detachment is like this flight: a movement of liberation, in which excesses are released and one chooses to carry only what is truly necessary to reach greater heights. To live like this is to allow yourself to flow through life with lightness, making room for what really matters - experiences, relationships, and a genuine connection with your own essence.

Attachment to material possessions often acts as an anchor that holds back and limits personal growth. The more we accumulate, the harder it becomes to perceive what is essential. Breaking this cycle of excessive accumulation opens doors to new possibilities. By getting rid of the superfluous, we create physical, mental, and emotional space for the new. This space allows new ideas to flourish, unexpected opportunities to arise, and deeper connections to be formed. The absence of excess brings clarity and focus, facilitating more conscious choices aligned with personal values.

Simplifying life, therefore, is not an act of deprivation, but of expansion. By eliminating the unnecessary, we gain time and energy to invest in what truly brings happiness and fulfillment. This process invites reflection on the true meaning of abundance. Far from being measured by the volume of accumulated goods, the concept of abundance manifests itself in experiences lived with authenticity and purpose. Each object left behind is a symbol of detachment, a firm step towards a fuller and more meaningful life.

Material detachment not only simplifies routine but also reduces stress and anxiety. The burden of maintaining, protecting, and accumulating objects brings with it constant worries. The maintenance of goods requires time, energy, and resources that could be directed towards more meaningful aspects of life. By letting go of this burden, an inner peace arises, a feeling of lightness and freedom that allows us to live in the present with more serenity. The focus shifts from having to being, providing emotional and mental balance.

This lightness achieved further strengthens gratitude. By valuing what we already have and recognizing the true riches of life - such as health, love, learning, and personal growth - we develop a more positive and fulfilling perspective. This state of gratitude not only generates contentment but also creates a continuous flow of abundance. Open minds and hearts attract new opportunities and enriching experiences, allowing prosperity to manifest naturally.

Connecting with inner abundance is one of the greatest gifts of detachment. When we are not attached to material possessions, it becomes easier to access talents, passions, and our own creativity. This connection with our essence reveals a wealth that does not depend on external factors. Living with authenticity and purpose strengthens self-confidence and autonomy, leading to a freer existence aligned with the true desires of the soul.

To cultivate material detachment, it is essential to start gradually. Small steps have a big impact. Separating objects that no longer have a use, such as clothes, books, or utensils, may seem simple, but it represents a significant movement of liberation. Each item donated or discarded is an invitation to reflect on what truly adds value to life. This process does not need to be abrupt; it should be conscious and constant, respecting the rhythm of each individual.

Practicing generosity is another powerful path to detachment. Donating objects to those in need or to charities transforms excess into opportunity. The act of sharing expands the perception of abundance and reinforces the idea that true wealth lies in flow - in giving and receiving - and not in the stagnation of goods. By giving away something that no longer serves us, we open space not only physically but also emotionally for the new.

Organizing spaces is a practical way to materialize detachment. Clean and organized environments reflect a clear and tranquil mind. By reviewing closets, drawers, and rooms in the house, we eliminate what is in excess and create an environment that favors harmony and well-being. This care for the space around us strengthens the connection with what really matters, making it easier to recognize what is essential.

Reflecting on consumption habits is a fundamental step in this process. Society often encourages unbridled consumption as the path to happiness. Questioning this pattern is crucial to developing a more conscious relationship with the material. Observing the triggers that lead to impulse purchases and prioritizing quality over quantity are attitudes that promote a more balanced life aligned with authentic values.

Valuing experiences over objects is a choice that transforms our relationship with the material world. Lived moments - trips, encounters, learning - leave deeper and more lasting marks than any physical good. These experiences enrich the soul, create emotional memories, and contribute to personal growth in a significant way.

Connection with nature also inspires detachment. The simplicity and harmony present in natural cycles show that life can be rich without excesses. Observing the flow of water, the growth of trees, and the flight of birds teaches us about the beauty of the essential. Spending time in nature reinforces the idea that less is more and that true abundance lies in simplicity.

Detaching from the past is another important step. We often keep objects laden with memories that no longer serve us. Photographs, letters, and material memories can become emotional anchors. Freeing ourselves from these ties allows us to fully live in the present and open the way to a lighter and freer future.

Simplifying finances is also a form of detachment. Organizing expenses, eliminating debt, and avoiding unnecessary purchases are practices that bring lightness and freedom. A balanced financial life favors more conscious choices and reduces worries, allowing us to focus on what truly brings fulfillment.

Adopting minimalism as a lifestyle is a practical expression of detachment. Living with less, but with purpose, brings clarity, freedom, and space for what really matters. This philosophy encourages the prioritization of the essential, allowing each choice to be made with intention and awareness.

By practicing material detachment continuously, we realize that small changes generate profound transformations. This process not only reorganizes the external environment but also impacts the way we deal with challenges and opportunities. The clarity gained strengthens the ability to make more assertive and conscious decisions, promoting balance and serenity.

Thus, material detachment becomes a path of self-knowledge and freedom. By letting go of the shackles of excessive consumption, we open space to live with more authenticity and purpose. This movement of detachment is reflected in a lighter and fuller life, where true abundance manifests itself in the experiences lived, in the bonds of affection, and in the inner peace that arises from living in a simple and meaningful way.

By incorporating material detachment into everyday life, it is possible to perceive how small changes generate profound and lasting impacts. This process does not require haste, but rather constancy and awareness in each choice. By recognizing what truly adds value to life, it becomes easier to let go of what is superfluous and give space to what promotes growth and well-being. Thus, each object left behind represents a step towards a more authentic, lighter life aligned with the true desires of the soul.

Over time, the practice of detachment transforms not only the physical environment but also the way we face challenges and opportunities. The clarity gained by simplifying life expands our perception of what is essential, strengthening our ability to make more conscious and assertive decisions. This new perspective allows us to deal with the ups and downs of life with more balance and serenity, valuing each experience as an opportunity for learning and evolution.

The journey of material detachment is, therefore, a path of self-knowledge and freedom. By letting go of the shackles that bind us to accumulation and unbridled consumption, we open space to live with more purpose and connection. This inner movement is reflected in a lighter existence, where true abundance manifests itself in the experiences lived, in the bonds of affection, and in the inner peace that arises from living in a simple and meaningful way.

Chapter 34
Simplicity and Minimalism

Adopting simplicity and minimalism is about taking conscious control of one's own life, choosing to live with intentionality and purpose. This path involves detaching from material excesses, unnecessary commitments, and stimuli that overload the mind, creating space for what truly matters. The practice of valuing the essential does not mean deprivation, but rather the pursuit of balance, authenticity, and well-being. When each object, activity, and relationship occupies a meaningful place, life gains lightness and clarity, allowing our true essence to flourish with more strength and naturalness.

This approach promotes an internal and external reorganization, favoring peace of mind and emotional freedom. The absence of accumulation and the elimination of distractions bring profound benefits, such as stress reduction, increased productivity, and the strengthening of personal connections. With less noise and clutter, it becomes easier to identify priorities, invest energy in relationships and projects that truly bring satisfaction, and nurture creativity. Simplicity is thus revealed as a path to a more meaningful life, aligned with one's own values and goals.

Living simply also opens space for gratitude and abundance. By appreciating what we already have and reducing the constant desire for more, we create a healthier relationship with consumption and time. This change in perspective contributes to a lighter and more harmonious routine, where there is more room for enriching experiences and true connections. Simplicity and minimalism transform existence into a journey of self-knowledge and freedom, allowing each choice to reflect what truly brings happiness and fulfillment.

Imagine a spacious house, illuminated by the soft light that enters through the open windows. Each room is organized harmoniously, where each object has a clear purpose and occupies its proper place. There are no excesses, no distractions, just space to breathe, to be. Simplicity and minimalism are like creating this environment not only around us but within ourselves. It is the conscious choice to eliminate excess, clutter, and noise, allowing vital energy to flow freely. This state of inner clarity paves the way for true abundance to manifest naturally.

Adopting simplicity and minimalism does not mean giving up comfort or living in deprivation. It is an intentional decision to value what truly matters, freeing oneself from the burden of excess and the constant search for more. This choice promotes balance, authenticity, and well-being, allowing every aspect of life - from the objects we own to the commitments we make - to reflect our deepest values. By aligning daily choices with what is essential, life gains lightness and clarity, and the true essence of who we are flourishes with more strength.

This internal and external reorganization brings numerous benefits. The absence of accumulation and the elimination of distractions reduce stress and anxiety, providing peace of mind and emotional freedom. With less noise around, it becomes easier to identify priorities, direct energy towards meaningful relationships and projects, and cultivate creativity. Living with less is not a sacrifice, but an opportunity to focus on what truly brings fulfillment. Simplicity is thus revealed as a path to a more aligned life with our goals and values.

Living simply also awakens gratitude and expands the perception of abundance. When we stop constantly seeking more and start valuing what we already have, we develop a healthier relationship with consumption and time. This change in perspective creates a more harmonious routine, where there is more room for enriching experiences and genuine connections. Simplicity and minimalism, then, not only organize life but transform it into a journey of self-knowledge and freedom, where each choice is a reflection of what truly brings happiness and fulfillment.

This lifestyle also frees up time and energy, precious resources that are often wasted on unnecessary activities, commitments, and possessions. When we rid ourselves of these distractions, we can dedicate ourselves more intensely to our dreams, passions, relationships, and our life purpose. This freedom gives us more focus and willingness to invest in what really matters, creating a feeling of lightness that permeates all areas of existence.

Furthermore, minimalism reduces stress and anxiety. Clutter, both physical and mental, overloads the mind, generating restlessness and fatigue. By opting for a simpler life, we slow down, calm our thoughts, and find a natural state of emotional balance. This serenity allows us to face challenges with more clarity and calmness, making life lighter and more satisfying.

With fewer distractions, focus and concentration increase significantly. The mind becomes clearer and more directed, facilitating productivity and allowing us to achieve goals more efficiently. This state of clarity also stimulates creativity, as an organized environment free of excess promotes imagination and the ability to find innovative solutions. Ideas flow more naturally when we are not overloaded by unnecessary stimuli.

By eliminating the superfluous, we strengthen the connection with our essence. This process of detachment invites us to revisit our values, priorities, and purpose. It is an opportunity to reconnect with who we truly are and what we desire for our lives. This reconnection guides us to more authentic choices aligned with our true goals, promoting a more coherent existence.

With this, gratitude intensifies. Living with less and with more purpose allows us to value every little blessing and see the true value of what we already have. This genuine appreciation brings us contentment and well-being, warding off the constant dissatisfaction that consumerism encourages. Simplicity opens space for abundance to manifest naturally, attracting opportunities and prosperity in all areas of life.

To cultivate this simplicity, the first step is to detach from excess material possessions. Donate, sell, or recycle objects, clothes, and utensils that are no longer useful or that do not bring joy. By keeping only the essentials, life becomes lighter and more meaningful. This process of detachment not only organizes the physical space but also promotes an internal reorganization, creating an environment conducive to well-being and mental clarity.

Organizing physical environments directly reflects on the mind. Organized spaces promote clarity, focus, and tranquility. By organizing closets, drawers, and rooms, we eliminate clutter and create a harmonious environment where energy can flow more lightly. This external harmony facilitates connection with what truly matters, creating a freer mental space for new ideas and projects.

Simplifying the routine is also essential. Eliminating unnecessary commitments and prioritizing activities that bring satisfaction allows for more productive and enjoyable days. This balance between doing and resting is fundamental to maintaining energy and motivation at healthy levels. Slowing down and living more calmly allows us to be present in each moment, appreciating the journey and not just the destination.

Practicing conscious consumption is another powerful way to integrate simplicity into life. Reflecting on consumption habits and opting for quality over quantity helps us avoid impulsive purchases and value what we acquire more. This behavior also contributes to a more sustainable life, reducing environmental impact and promoting more ethical consumption.

Digital minimalism is equally important. Reducing the time spent on social media, emails, and digital distractions allows for a deeper connection with the real world. Disconnecting from information overload helps us reconnect with ourselves and what truly matters, bringing more balance and mental clarity.

Living with simplicity and minimalism is not a change that happens overnight, but a continuous process of conscious choices. Each decision to eliminate excess and value the essential contributes to a fuller and more meaningful life. It is a path of self-knowledge and freedom, where true value lies not in what you own, but in what you live.

In the end, simplicity and minimalism are revealed as transformative choices. This constant movement of detachment and reconnection with the essential not only relieves the burden of excess but also strengthens presence, gratitude, and freedom. Living with less becomes living with more: more meaning, more lightness, and more harmony.

By adopting simplicity and minimalism, we create an internal environment conducive to the flourishing of authenticity and peace. This path is not just about reducing material excesses but about building a lighter and more present mindset, where each choice is made consciously. This balance provides not only clarity in goals but also strengthens the connection with the present moment, allowing us to appreciate the small daily joys with more depth.

With fewer distractions and unnecessary commitments, it becomes possible to dedicate ourselves more genuinely to interpersonal relationships and activities that bring true meaning. This renewed space in the mind and heart opens doors to richer and more authentic experiences, where quality prevails over quantity. Thus, cultivating simplicity becomes a continuous exercise in self-knowledge, where each step is guided by personal values and the pursuit of balance.

In the end, simplicity and minimalism are revealed as transformative choices, capable of leading to a fuller and more satisfying life. This constant process of detachment and reconnection with the essential not only relieves the burden of excess but also strengthens presence, gratitude, and freedom. Thus, living with less becomes living with more: more meaning, more lightness, and more harmony.

Chapter 35
Inner Abundance

True abundance is born within, like a silent and powerful force that sustains every aspect of life. It is about recognizing and valuing the immense emotional, spiritual, and mental wealth that dwells within you, regardless of external circumstances. This state of inner fullness is reflected in positive thoughts, balanced attitudes, and a deep connection with your own essence. From this awareness, it becomes possible to live with more serenity, confidence, and gratitude, allowing prosperity to flow naturally in all areas of life. Inner abundance is not something to be conquered, but rather awakened, as it already exists as an intrinsic part of who you are.

This inner wealth is revealed in the ability to find peace amidst challenges, love in everyday relationships, and joy in small daily achievements. By strengthening the connection with your values, talents, and purposes, you access an inexhaustible source of energy that drives personal and emotional growth. This state of contentment does not depend on material possessions or external validation, but rather on the harmony between mind, body, and spirit. When the perception of yourself expands, the vision of life also transforms, allowing you to see opportunities where there were once limitations and cultivate gratitude for each experience lived.

Developing this inner abundance requires an attentive inward gaze, through practices that favor self-knowledge, self-love, and acceptance. This continuous process involves caring for yourself with compassion, forgiving old wounds, and valuing each step of your personal journey. By nurturing positive thoughts and making space for genuine feelings of gratitude and generosity, you create a fertile inner environment for peace and happiness. Thus, inner abundance becomes the solid foundation for a full life, where each choice is guided by harmony and each action reflects the prosperity that already dwells in your heart.

Imagine an artesian well hidden in the depths of the earth, from which springs crystal clear and pure water, incessant and abundant, without ever being affected by storms or aridity that may exist on the surface. Such is inner abundance: an inexhaustible source of emotional and spiritual wealth that emanates from the core of being, nourishing and strengthening every aspect of life. This constant and silent energy remains intact, even in the face of adversity, offering sustenance and balance. It does not depend on external factors, but flows naturally, guiding thoughts, emotions, and actions in a harmonious way.

This deep connection with one's own essence becomes the foundation of true happiness. When one understands that fulfillment is not in possessions or social approval, but in the ability to embrace one's own authenticity, one discovers a state of constant serenity.

Happiness becomes cultivated internally, nurtured by peace of mind, gratitude, and unconditional love. This feeling of contentment does not arise from external achievements, but from intimacy with the values, passions, and purposes that shape each individual's identity.

Awakening this inner abundance requires a journey of sincere and profound self-knowledge. It is necessary to explore thoughts, emotions, and beliefs with courage, diving into the most intimate layers of one's own existence. This search allows access to hidden talents, forgotten passions, and fundamental values that guide choices and shape character. From this understanding, a sense of belonging and authenticity emerges, as if each inner discovery were an essential piece in the puzzle of self-realization.

At the heart of this journey, self-love flourishes as a solid foundation. Recognizing one's own worth, with all qualities and imperfections, is an act of compassion and respect for oneself. This genuine love strengthens self-confidence and creates an internal environment conducive to growth and happiness. Accepting oneself fully, without judgment, allows one to embrace one's own humanity and walk more lightly through life, free from the shackles of excessive self-criticism.

Gratitude, in turn, acts as a powerful transformer of perception. By practicing gratitude daily, every detail of life takes on a new glow. Small blessings, often unnoticed, come to be recognized as precious gifts. Giving thanks for relationships, opportunities, and even challenges expands the ability to see the abundance that already exists. This positive mindset opens doors to enriching experiences, creating a continuous cycle of inner prosperity.

Forgiveness emerges as a bridge to emotional freedom. Freeing oneself from the weight of grudges and resentment, forgiving oneself and others, dissolves the barriers that prevent the flow of inner peace. Forgiveness does not mean forgetting or justifying, but rather choosing not to carry the burden of the past any longer. This decision opens space for genuine feelings of love and understanding to flourish, allowing abundance to flow freely in life.

Meditation presents itself as an essential practice to access this inner source of wealth. In the silence of the mind, away from external noise, it is possible to find clarity and serenity. The connection with the present moment, provided by meditation, reveals the peace and wisdom that have always been there, hidden under the layers of incessant thoughts. This state of inner balance strengthens the perception of abundance already existing, creating a fertile space for happiness to flourish.

Mindfulness practices reinforce this connection with the now. By paying attention to the present without judgment, each experience becomes more vivid and meaningful. Feeling the texture of a leaf, the aroma of coffee, or the warmth of the sun on your skin are simple moments that, when fully lived, reveal the richness of everyday life. This conscious presence nourishes the feeling of completeness and dissolves anxiety about the past or future.

Nature also plays a fundamental role in this reconnection process. Being in contact with natural environments, feeling the wind, listening to the sound of water, or observing the movement of trees brings a silent and profound renewal. Nature inspires and teaches about cycles, resilience, and balance, awakening in human beings a sense of belonging to the whole and to the abundance of creation.

Furthermore, the cultivation of virtues such as compassion, generosity, patience, and humility enriches the soul. Practicing these qualities not only strengthens character, but also expands the perception of inner prosperity. Compassion connects hearts, generosity opens paths, patience brings wisdom, and humility allows one to grow with authenticity. These virtues are reflected in daily actions, creating a cycle of well-being and harmony with the world.

Acceptance emerges as an invitation to lightness. Accepting the circumstances of life, with its uncertainties and challenges, frees one from resistance and allows one to flow more naturally. This acceptance is not resignation, but an understanding that each experience, pleasant or not, brings with it a valuable lesson. With serenity, it is possible to embrace changes and challenges as opportunities for evolution.

Self-care complements this path, being an expression of love and respect for one's own existence. Nourishing the body with healthy food, exercising, sleeping well, and setting aside time for leisure are concrete ways to honor one's own life. This integral care sustains physical, emotional, and mental balance, strengthening the foundation for inner abundance to manifest fully.

When this abundance is expressed in everyday life, relationships are transformed. Bonds become more authentic and profound, based on respect and empathy. From the recognition of one's own inner wealth, it becomes possible to see and value the emotional wealth of others, creating more harmonious and lasting connections.

In the professional environment, this abundance drives performance with purpose and creativity. Working with passion and authenticity opens space for innovation and achievement. Success ceases to be just an external goal and becomes a reflection of the genuine expression of talents and values, making the work environment more rewarding and productive.

In finances, this mentality promotes balance. Money is managed with wisdom and responsibility, not as a source of anxiety, but as a resource that supports a life aligned with one's own values. This avoids excesses and waste, bringing security and financial freedom.

In health, positive thoughts and healthy practices strengthen the body and mind. Well-being becomes a natural priority, promoting vitality and energy to live fully. In spirituality, this abundance deepens the connection with the divine, expanding faith and gratitude for life.

Thus, inner abundance is revealed as a constant flow of love, peace, and purpose, illuminating each step of the journey. It is an invitation to live with more lightness, confidence, and gratitude, allowing true prosperity to manifest itself in every aspect of existence.

When inner abundance becomes an essential part of your being, each experience lived takes on a new meaning. Challenges cease to be obstacles and become opportunities for growth, while achievements, however small, become genuine celebrations of life. This perspective transforms the way you relate to yourself and the world, guiding your choices with more wisdom and balance. From this solid foundation, the path to personal and collective fulfillment becomes clearer, flowing naturally in harmony with your values and purposes.

This inner transformation also reflects in the way you impact the environment around you. The positive energy generated by inner abundance inspires and infects other people, creating cycles of kindness, cooperation, and prosperity. Small gestures of generosity and understanding multiply, contributing to more welcoming environments and more authentic relationships. Thus, the pursuit of fulfillment ceases to be a solitary goal and expands, promoting collective well-being and strengthening bonds of empathy and solidarity.

Allowing yourself to live inner abundance is, therefore, an invitation to honor your own journey with love, acceptance, and confidence. Each step taken towards self-knowledge, caring for the body, and spiritual connection nourishes this inexhaustible source of fullness. And it is in this state of balance and harmony that life reveals itself in its richest and truest form, leading you to an existence where peace, prosperity, and happiness are not distant goals, but realities present in every moment.

Chapter 36
Sharing Abundance

Sharing abundance represents the most authentic expression of prosperity, in which generosity transforms into a powerful link of connection and collective growth. When one recognizes that resources, talents, and achievements can be amplified through sharing, a continuous flow of prosperity is created that benefits everyone. This movement transcends the simple act of donating material goods; it involves cultivating an open and receptive mindset, capable of transforming small actions into great impacts. Abundance is not limited to what one possesses, but manifests fully when shared with genuine intention, strengthening bonds, inspiring change, and expanding opportunities for everyone around.

By adopting the practice of sharing, a network of support and solidarity is strengthened that drives mutual growth. Generosity nourishes relationships, strengthens emotional bonds, and promotes a culture of collaboration, in which each gesture contributes to a more harmonious and balanced environment. This sincere exchange not only meets immediate needs, but also creates a solid foundation for building a more just and compassionate society. The impact of these actions reverberates in multiple spheres of life, promoting emotional well-being, security, and mutual trust. Thus, sharing abundance becomes a natural path to generating continuous and sustainable prosperity.

Each act of sharing carries with it the seed of transformation. Whether through dedicated time, words of encouragement, or material resources, every expression of generosity contributes to strengthening the current of abundance. This flow expands as it inspires others to adopt similar attitudes, creating an upward spiral of cooperation and collective growth. True abundance lies in the awareness that there is always something valuable to offer and that, by distributing what one has to offer, space is opened to receive even more. This virtuous cycle not only transforms lives individually, but also positively impacts the world as a whole, promoting a more prosperous and balanced reality.

Imagine a long, welcoming table covered with a linen tablecloth, where steaming, colorful dishes are lovingly arranged. Around it, people from different backgrounds and journeys gather, exchanging smiles and warm words. The aroma of food mingles with the lightness of laughter and the sparkle in the eyes of those who share not only the food, but also moments of true connection. This scenario vividly translates the meaning of sharing abundance. More than dividing material resources, it is about opening space for the other, inviting them to participate in our prosperity and celebrate the abundance of life together.

This act of inviting someone to the table of abundance is a profound expression of gratitude. When we share what we have, we acknowledge the blessings we have received and show appreciation for the achievements we have made. This sincere recognition resonates as a silent declaration to the universe, affirming that we are ready to receive even more. Generosity, in this context, is not just an act of giving, but also a way of honoring the present and preparing the heart to welcome new opportunities. The universe, sensitive to the vibration of gratitude, responds with the expansion of prosperity, creating a continuous flow of blessings.

This practice also raises personal vibration. By acting with generosity, feelings of joy, love, and compassion intensify, impregnating each action with a high and positive energy. This elevated vibrational state acts as a beacon, attracting enriching experiences and strengthening attunement with the frequency of abundance. Each gesture of sharing emanates waves of well-being, creating an environment where positivity spreads and inspires new attitudes. Thus, sharing becomes a way of nourishing one's own spirit while contributing to the harmony around.

The impact of sharing goes beyond the isolated act; it triggers a virtuous cycle. Each demonstration of generosity inspires others to do the same, forming a continuous chain of cooperation and solidarity. This flow of giving and receiving strengthens social bonds and expands collective abundance. The awareness that there is always something valuable to offer - be it time, knowledge, or simple words of support - transforms the way we relate to the world. By letting go of the fear of scarcity and trusting in the abundance of life, we create a support network where everyone prospers.

In relationships, the act of sharing is revealed as a powerful link of strengthening. Offering quality time, small gestures of affection, or support in difficult times solidifies emotional bonds. These actions generate meaningful memories and deepen emotional connections. Generosity, when cultivated spontaneously, not only nourishes existing relationships, but also attracts new connections, based on trust and empathy. Sincere exchange becomes a solid foundation for building lasting and true relationships.

In addition to the personal impact, sharing abundance contributes directly to transforming the world. Small gestures, such as donating financial resources, time, or talents, reverberate in positive social changes. When a person decides to support a cause, help someone, or contribute their knowledge, this attitude multiplies, creating waves of transformation. The world becomes more just and compassionate, and each individual contribution becomes part of a collective movement of evolution and balance. Thus, generosity not only improves individual lives, but also shapes a more caring society.

There are several ways to share abundance, and each carries its own unique value. Financial donation, for example, allows you to support social projects, NGOs, and people in vulnerable situations. This act of detachment not only meets urgent needs, but also reinforces in the donor the sense of purpose and belonging to a greater cause. Volunteering, on the other hand, transforms skills and time into tools for positive impact. By dedicating efforts to help communities or individuals, empathy and genuine connection with the community are developed.

Another powerful way is the donation of material goods. Clothes, food, books, or toys that are no longer useful can be essential for other people. This simple gesture not only meets immediate needs, but also encourages a culture of conscious consumption, in which excess is redistributed responsibly. Sharing meals, in turn, carries a special symbolism. Inviting someone to share food goes beyond physical nourishment; it is an invitation to celebrate life, strengthen bonds, and create emotional memories.

Offering help, even in small gestures, is equally transformative. Listening carefully, helping with a task, or simply being present can make an immeasurable difference in someone's life. This genuine care creates an environment of mutual support, where empathy and respect are cultivated. Sharing knowledge is also a powerful form of contribution. The exchange of knowledge, whether through mentoring, lectures, or informal conversations, broadens horizons, inspires new paths, and strengthens the network of collective learning.

Dedicating quality time is perhaps one of the most authentic expressions of generosity. Being fully present, listening carefully, and showing sincere interest nourishes emotional bonds and creates a space of trust and acceptance. In addition, spreading joy and positivity through words of encouragement or gestures of kindness has the power to brighten someone's day. These simple actions trigger a chain of well-being that spreads silently, helping to make the world lighter and more hopeful.

For the act of sharing to be even more impactful, it is essential to act from the heart. Authenticity, detachment, and genuine generosity make each gesture meaningful. It is not about quantity, but about the quality of intention behind the action. Small actions taken with love and consistency have the power to transform realities. In addition, finding creative ways to contribute can expand the reach of generosity. Innovative projects, community actions, and social initiatives are ways to spread abundance in a unique and transformative way.

Finally, consistency is key to keeping this flow of abundance active. Making generosity part of the routine, with daily or regular sharing practices, integrates this value into the way of life. Each action, however small, reinforces the culture of solidarity and cooperation. By sharing frequently, you inspire others to do the same, creating a solid network of support and prosperity.

Thus, sharing abundance becomes more than a simple act: it is a life choice. A conscious decision to live in harmony with the world and with those around us. This continuous practice not only transforms those who receive, but mainly those who offer, cultivating a lasting state of contentment, fullness, and true connection with the natural flow of prosperity.

By integrating the act of sharing into the daily routine, one realizes that abundance is not a finite resource, but an energy that is renewed with each gesture of generosity. This constant practice transforms not only those who receive, but mainly those who offer, promoting a state of contentment and fullness. The awareness that small actions can trigger major changes strengthens confidence in the collective impact and fuels the desire to contribute continuously to the common good.

This perspective broadens the understanding of prosperity, detaching it from individual accumulation and connecting it to the constant flow of exchange and collaboration. True wealth is revealed in the ability to recognize the value of relationships, time, and attention dedicated to others. By acting with generosity and empathy, a resilient support network is built, capable of facing challenges and celebrating achievements together, creating a solid foundation for a more prosperous future.

Thus, sharing abundance is not just an isolated gesture, but a conscious choice to live in harmony with the world around us. This path of generosity transforms reality and inspires new possibilities for collective growth. By cultivating this practice, the commitment to a more balanced existence is reinforced, where prosperity expands naturally and touches everyone's lives in a positive and lasting way.

Epilogue

Upon reaching the end of this journey, a truth is clearly revealed: abundance is not a destination, but a continuous path, a daily choice that manifests itself in every thought, word, and action. You have traveled paths that challenged old beliefs, unveiled the veils that hid your potential, and now carry with you a new perception of what it means to live fully.

But this journey does not end here. On the contrary, it is now that it truly begins.

Everything that has been explored in these pages - the power of positive thoughts, the strength of affirmations, the practice of creative visualization, the understanding of the Law of Attraction, overcoming limiting beliefs, diving into self-knowledge, and the search for inner healing - forms a solid foundation. A fertile ground, ready for you to plant the seeds of the life you wish to cultivate.

You have already awakened.

Now is the time to sustain this awakening. True transformation happens when knowledge becomes practice, when inspiration translates into action. Each teaching absorbed here is a tool waiting to be used, not sporadically, but as an integral part of your routine, silently shaping your reality.

Perhaps you have already felt subtle shifts in your perception or experienced small synchronicities throughout this reading. These are signs that the energy of abundance has already begun to flow, responding to your new vibration. Recognize these moments as confirmations that you are on the right path.

But remember: the journey of abundance requires consistency. Old beliefs may try to return, challenges